Tiger Management

Throughout the last several decades, Korean companies have entered the world markets in a wide range of manufacturing industries, with great success. How did they achieve this exceptional performance? This book uncovers the secret of their success through a comprehensive analysis of the Korean management system which is labeled Tiger Management. It explains to an international audience how it has developed, why it works so well, and what non-Koreans can learn from it.

The book analyzes the management of Korean firms from three different perspectives. First, a historical perspective is applied by showing how Tiger Management has emerged and how it has been continuously advanced over the last fifty years. The breathtaking stories of how Korean companies, seemingly coming from nowhere, have challenged their Western and Japanese competitors on the world markets are told. Second, the cornerstones of Tiger Management are analyzed from a functional viewpoint, showing that the success of Korean companies rests on a smart combination of business strategy, leadership, and human resource management practices. Finally, the present and future of Tiger Management are discussed by showing how Korean companies have adapted to changes in their business environment at home and abroad, and what non-Korean companies can learn from their Korean rivals.

The book gives an up-to-date analysis of Korean management practices from a global perspective. It identifies the success factors of Korean companies: long-term, aggressive, and persistent business planning; speed; flexibility; strong leadership; strong teamwork; and high investment into human skills and capabilities. It illustrates how these management practices complement each other and provides non-Korean companies with signposts as to how they can adopt them.

Martin Hemmert is Professor of International Business at Korea University Business School in Seoul. Previously, he has held teaching or research positions at the University of Cologne, University of Duisburg-Essen, Hitotsubashi University, DIJ Tokyo, and the National University of Singapore. He has published six books and numerous articles in peer-reviewed international journals. His current research interests include the management of Korean firms and international comparative research on technology alliances.

Tiger Management

Korean companies on world markets

Martin Hemmert

Routledge
Taylor & Francis Group

LONDON AND NEW YORK

First published 2012
by Routledge
2 Park Square, Milton Park, Abingdon, Oxon, OX14 4RN

Simultaneously published in the USA and Canada
by Routledge
711 Third Avenue, New York, NY 10017

Routledge is an imprint of the Taylor & Francis Group, an informa business

British Library Cataloguing in Publication Data
A catalogue record for this book is available from the British Library

Library of Congress Cataloging in Publication Data
Hemmert, Martin, 1964-
   Tiger Management: Korean companies on world markets/Martin Hemmert.
   p. cm. – (Routledge studies in the modern world economy; 108)
   Includes bibliographical references and index.
   1. Management–Korea (South) 2. Corporate culture–Korea (South)
   3. Business enterprises–Korea (South) I. Title.
HD70.K6H46 2012
658–dc23   2012002822

ISBN: 978-0-415-66418-9 (hbk)
ISBN: 978-0-415-53720-9 (pbk)
ISBN: 978-0-203-11067-6 (ebk)

Typeset in Times New Roman
by Sunrise Setting Ltd, Torquay, UK

Dedicated to Mi-chan and Frank

Contents

Figures and tables

Figures

Tables

Preface

This book is the result of an intellectual journey of almost eight years. Soon after I moved to Korea in early 2004, I noticed an interesting discrepancy. On the one hand, it became clear to me that many Korean companies are doing very well in global competition – much better than I was previously aware of. On the other hand, many observers, Korean and foreign, continued to talk about all the problems of Korean businesses and what they should do to shed inferior practices and follow global standards. Partially, this may have to do with the aftermath of the Asian financial crisis, a time when the weaknesses of Korean companies were brutally exposed. It may also be related to the tendency among Koreans to be very strict and critical with themselves. This is a healthy attitude in order to avoid complacency, but it can unintentionally also result in an undervalued outside image. The whole situation was an intriguing reversal from what I had experienced in Japan in the 1990s. Back then, many observers emphasized the virtues of Japanese style management, whereas Japanese companies often struggled to stay globally competitive.

I began to study Korean management practices, and their cultural and economic context, systematically. It became a very fascinating research topic, as I continued to discover ever new aspects of how Korean companies are managed and organized, and how these practices help them gain competitive strength. Eventually, I decided to summarize my findings in this book.

At the time of writing, the global prospects of Korean companies and business groups look brighter than ever. They are continuously outperforming their Western and Japanese rivals. Some of them have emerged as global leaders, which are highly respected or even feared by their competitors. Yet, my general observation is that most non-Korean businesspeople are still struggling to understand Korean management practices, and how these practices help companies to be so competitive. I hope that this piece may help a bit with gaining a better understanding of Korean companies and their management systems. I also hope that it helps in giving Korean firms and their managers the international recognition they deserve. It will be highly beneficial if non-Korean companies seriously study what they can learn from their Korean counterparts.

Many people have supported me with this project through formal and informal exchanges in various ways. I am grateful to my colleagues at Korea University Business School for sharing their insights on Korean businesses and to the School itself for providing me with an excellent research environment. I would also like to express my gratitude to all the managers of Korean firms who have granted me interviews, and to all my friends and colleagues who provided me with valuable feedback on this research in various stages. I am particularly indebted to Myeong-gyu Ahn, Tony Garrett, Hyun Hwoi Ha, Taeksoo Kim, Josef Meilinger, Joachim Nowak, Felix Reimann, Frank Rövekamp, and Wolfgang Slawinski. Jaejin Kim and Youngwoo Lee provided excellent research assistance over several years. Special thanks go to Patrick Reinmoeller for inspiring me to write this piece. Finally, I would like to thank Routledge Editor Yongling Lam and her team for their efforts to turn my manuscript into a book.

Martin Hemmert
Tokyo
December 2011

Note on Korean names and Korean language references

In this book, Korean names are written according to Korean convention, with last names given first and first names thereafter (e.g. Park Chung-hee instead of Chung-hee Park).

References written in Korean language are listed first in English translation, followed by the original titles in Korean.

List of abbreviations

ASEAN	Association of Southeast Asian Nations
CEO	Chief Executive Officer
DRAM	Dynamic Random Access Memory
FDI	Foreign Direct Investment
GDP	Gross Domestic Product
IMF	International Monetary Fund
KRW	South Korean Won
LED	Light-emitting Diode
MBA	Master of Business Administration
MBO	Management by Objectives
OECD	Organization for Economic Co-operation and Development
OEM	Original Equipment Manufacturer
R&D	Research and Development
SME	Small- and Medium-sized Enterprise

Korean words

	Writing in Korean	Writing in Chinese characters	English translation
chaebol	재벌	財閥	business group
chung	충	忠	loyalty
dongban seongchang	동반성장	同伴成長	co-prosperity
hallyu	한류	韓流	Korean wave
inwha	인화	人和	harmony
jeong	정	情	human affection
jeongdo kyeongyeong	정도경영	正道経営	integrity management
palli palli	빨리 빨리		quickly quickly
sahoon	사훈	社訓	company motto
yangban	양반	両班	noblemen

Part I
Introduction

1 Tiger Management

The growth and rising competitiveness of Korean firms

> The mother was returning from the village one day when she was encountered by a tiger perched on a hill demanding a rice cake in exchange for sparing her life. She gave it to him and the tiger went away, only to appear before her at the next hill; this time demanding two rice cakes. She gave him the cakes, only to find him again on the third hill, this time asking for four rice cakes. When the mother finally ran out of rice cakes to feed him, the tiger threatened to devour her.
>
> The mother pleaded, saying she was the sole mother of two children. Upon hearing this, the tiger's hunger grew even more vicious. He devoured the mother and then took on her clothing as a disguise. He then made his way to the house where he knew the children awaited.
>
> From the Korean legend "The Sun and the Moon"[1]

Tigers are fierce animals. So are Korean companies, particularly when they compete with you. Over the last several decades, Korean companies, seemingly coming from nowhere, have built strong or dominant positions in a wide range of global industries ranging from semiconductors and mobile phones to automobiles and ships. None of their American, European, or Japanese competitors could stop them, and some were forced out of business. It therefore appears high time to gain a better understanding of the companies' miraculous rise and to consider what can be learned from them.

Korean management: basket case or role model?

Following the long-lasting economic boom in East Asia, the management of companies in some leading economies of this region has attracted significant global interest. After the emergence of Japanese companies on the world markets, Japanese management techniques and practices have been studied intensively by international scholars.[2] Japanese management remains an established research topic, even though the enthusiasm about this topic has somewhat cooled following the stagnation of the Japanese economy since the 1990s. More recently, in the wake of China's transformation into a global manufacturing powerhouse, many observers have also become interested in the management of Chinese firms.[3]

Compared with these two countries, South Korea (subsequently: Korea), as the third largest East Asian economy, has received relatively little attention by researchers and managers. Korean management has not been a topic of high interest.

This situation was not always the same. Noticing the rise of Korea as an industrial power and the global emergence of its business groups (*chaebols*), a certain interest among business researchers grew up from the late 1980s and throughout the 1990s. Alice Amsden labeled Korea as "Asia's next giant."[4] Gerardo Ungson and his co-authors emphasized the dynamic transformation and globalization of the Korean economy and Korean firms.[5] In general, while not becoming a mainstream topic in business research, the management of Korean firms received some attention because of the Korean economic miracle that led observers to ask for its origins.

Then, however, the Asian financial crisis struck Korea in 1997. Its currency and stock market crashed, and the government had to seek the IMF's (International Monetary Fund) assistance to escape default. Many Korean companies went bankrupt and had to be reorganized or were taken over by foreign firms. Not surprisingly, the crisis also changed the overall perception of Korean management. The structure and organization of *chaebols* were commonly blamed for not being up to the standards of an advanced country and being one of the underlying reasons for the country's economic crash. Korean management became a synonym for bad corporate governance, lack of transparency and professionalism, and reckless diversification. Korean and foreign observers agreed that fundamental changes had to be made in the management of Korean firms to allow them to restore their competitiveness and prevent further disasters in the future.[6] In other words, "Korean management" became almost a basket case in the eyes of researchers and analysts – a stark example of what must be avoided in the management of companies in emerging economies.

This perception prevailed even after Korea had overcome its economic and financial crisis. Korean companies are mostly analyzed regarding the degree to which they have been successfully restructured and whether their fundamental weaknesses have been eliminated or not.[7] In other words, many observers still believe that Korean companies and managers need to continue their homework of shedding bad and inferior practices from previous times and converging to superior "global standards."

Is Korean management, then, a basket case? The central argument of this book is that it is not. Rather, it will be shown that Korean management has much genuine strength that gives the country's firms and business groups a high amount of international competitiveness. Furthermore, it will be suggested that management researchers and practitioners should examine Korean management from a different viewpoint. Rather than focusing only on the question of "How can Korean firms improve their management systems?" it should be seriously asked "What can we learn and adopt from Korean management?" In other words, Korean management, at least regarding certain aspects, could be regarded as a role model for the management of firms in other countries, particularly in emerging economies.

The distinctive and widely successful management of Korean firms is labeled as Tiger Management in this book. Four East Asian economies are often described as "tiger"[8] or "dragon"[9] economies: Korea, Taiwan, Hong Kong, and Singapore. However, whereas the dragon is primarily a Chinese emblem, and can therefore be broadly associated with Taiwan, Hong Kong, and Singapore, which all have populations with predominantly ethnic Chinese origin, the tiger is mostly used as a Korean national symbol.[10] Moreover, it also embodies many features of Korean management that will be discussed in this book: speed, aggressiveness, dynamism, and bravery. Therefore, the management of Korean firms is subsequently referred to as Tiger Management.

The performance of Korean firms and the case for Tiger Management

A review of the recent performance of Korean firms is instrumental to make the case for Tiger Management. As can be seen from Figure 1.1, whereas the largest Korean

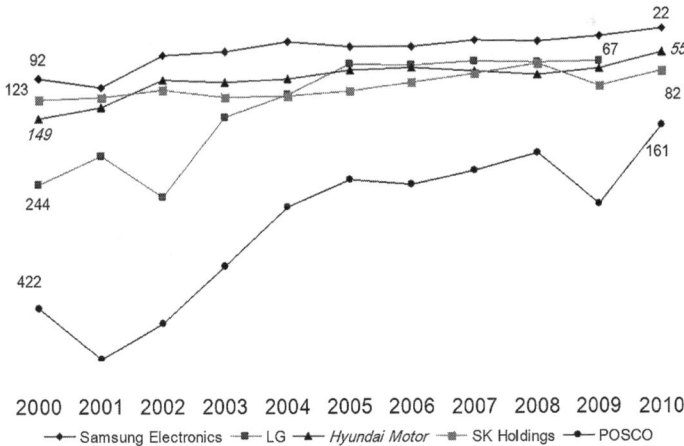

Figure 1.1 Ranking of leading Korean firms in Fortune 500.

Source: CNN Money, Fortune Global 500.

Note: Data for LG were not reported on the group level for 2010.

firms have entered the ranks of the globally largest 500 companies since the 1990s, their ranking has continuously improved since the turn of the millennium. This clearly indicates the global importance Korean firms have gained as they have not just grown, but grown relatively faster than their rivals from other countries.

However, the rise of Korean companies can also be observed on the level of individual industries and firms. Many Korean companies have advanced to leading or strong positions in a number of important manufacturing industries.

One well-known case is the electronics industry. Here, two Korean firms, Samsung Electronics and LG Electronics, have emerged in recent years from second tier OEMs (original equipment manufacturers) to leading global players. Samsung Electronics was founded in 1969 when Samsung group expanded into the electronics business. In its early days, it depended on technological aid from Japan's Sanyo and concentrated on producing relatively simple electronic products such as TVs, refrigerators, and microwave ovens. Whereas the company entered the semiconductor business some time in the late 1970s, it achieved global leadership in the memory chip industry as early as in 1992 and has never given it up since then.[11] Samsung and LG are holding the positions number two and three in the world market for mobile phones.[12] LG Electronics' success, while not being as spectacular as Samsung's, is also quite remarkable. It was founded in 1958 as GoldStar and was the first Korean producer of radios, TVs, refrigerators, and other household electronics. In recent years, the company has become a strong global player in the consumer electronics industry and holds the world number one market share in various product categories, such as optical storage and refrigerators.[13]

The success of Korean companies is not limited to the electronics industry, however. Another well-known example is Korea's leading carmaker, Hyundai Motor. It was established in 1967 and initially assembled vehicles for Ford under a licensing agreement before beginning manufacture of its own models in 1976. Thereafter, Hyundai Motor group has been steadily growing throughout the last decades and is now the fourth largest automobile company in the world.[14] It is not only dominating the domestic Korean market, but also becoming more and more successful in North America, Europe, and elsewhere. Recent major investments have secured the company a strong foothold in large emerging markets such as China and India.

Another strong Korean national champion is POSCO in the steel industry. Founded by the Korean government in 1968, the company commenced integrated steel production in 1973. Now, it is the world's third largest steel producer.[15] More remarkably, the company has transformed itself from a government owned business to a dynamic global player throughout the last ten years. It has strengthened its competitiveness through breakthrough innovations in steelmaking that allow major reductions in operating cost and, at the same time, more environmentally friendly production processes. In contrast to most steelmakers from other countries, which tend to produce solely in their home countries or internationalize through M&As (mergers and acquisitions) only, POSCO is aggressively investing in production facilities in India and China to reduce cost and take advantage of access to abundantly available raw materials.

Korean companies are also dominating the global shipbuilding industry.[16] Operations began only in the 1970s, but Korean shipbuilders now hold a global market share of more than thirty percent.[17] Whereas government support played an important role during the early development stage, the subsequent gains in competitiveness are mostly the result of accumulated technological skills and the creation of innovative clusters. In these clusters, Korean shipbuilders benefit from linkages with many sophisticated suppliers and specialized research institutes.[18]

Taken together, it becomes clear that Korean companies, which unanimously started from very humble beginnings in the mid twentieth century, have gained strong global positions in a broad set of skill- und technology-intensive manufacturing industries. However, these companies have not just grown big. Most of them are also very profitable. An outstanding example is again Samsung Electronics. The company's net annual profits amounted to between five and ten percent of its sales during recent years, with 2010 being a record year when net profits of 16.1 trillion KRW (South Korean Won), equivalent to approximately US$14 billion were achieved.[19] Other Korean companies also regularly post healthy profits.

Moreover, the achievements of Korean firms are not limited to member companies of large business groups. In fact, there has always been a lot of vibrant entrepreneurship in Korea throughout recent decades, and nowadays big business groups have all had their origins in such humble start-ups. And there is more to come. Since the 1990s, an increasing number of second and third generation Korean companies are appearing on the world markets. A recent survey of small- and medium-sized Korean venture firms revealed that more than forty percent of them have internationalized their business, with many of them directly investing abroad.[20] Often, they are focusing on high-tech products and services. Whereas some of them – as everywhere – eventually do not succeed, others show a truly remarkable dynamism and growth.

The global emergence of Korean firms is also not limited to the manufacturing sector. A respectable software industry has developed since the 1990s, and many of its competitive companies are now globalizing their business.[21] Another field where Korea has grown particularly strong is entertainment, including TV dramas and pop music. As exemplified by the term "*hallyu*" (Korean wave), many actors and their companies have enjoyed great global success since the turn of the millennium.[22]

In sum, it can be clearly seen that Korean companies, large and small ones, have consistently shown an outstanding performance over the last several decades. Typically starting with almost no resources from very small beginnings, they grew big and became leading global players very quickly. Often dismissed by competitors for their allegedly inferior management, products, and technologies, they have repeatedly outperformed these rivals in product after product and market after market. These achievements, which often look almost like miracles for outside observers, are also reflected on the macroeconomic level. Between 1962 and 2007, Korea's annual per capita income increased by a surprising 250 times from US$82 to more than US$20,000,[23] showing the rapid transformation of an extremely poor, backward agricultural economy to a rich, advanced industrial country.

The stunning performance of many Korean companies warrants a closer look at how they are managed and organized. What are the cultural and institutional foundations of Tiger Management, and to what extent can Tiger Management become a role model for the management of companies elsewhere? These issues will all be addressed in the following chapters.

The structure of this book

Subsequently, Tiger Management will be analyzed in greater detail. Chapters 2 through 6 will provide a historical and evolutionary review of Korean companies and Tiger Management. In Chapter 2, the cultural and institutional roots of Korean capitalism are discussed. Thereafter, the early growth stages of Korean companies will be analyzed in Chapter 3, whereas Chapter 4 will focus on their rise to the international stage and their competitive battles on the world markets. Chapter 5 will give a review of their struggles during the Asian economic crisis of the late 1990s, and Chapter 6 focuses on their recent advances after having overcome this crisis.

Thereafter, the essence of Tiger Management will be analyzed from a functional perspective in Chapters 7 through 9. The discussion will be concentrated on managerial fields in which the distinctive characteristics of Tiger Management can be observed most clearly. Chapter 7 will focus on corporate and competitive strategies, Chapter 8 on leadership, and Chapter 9 on human resource management. It will be shown that in all these three areas, Korean companies have developed a particular management style that enabled their great success.

Finally, the present and future of Tiger Management will be discussed. Specifically, Chapter 10 will look at the challenge of globalization, focusing on the question of how Tiger Management can be sustained when Korean companies are globalizing. Chapter 11 will discuss the issue of sustainability of Tiger Management in the wake of the cultural, societal, and economic changes in Korea itself. Chapter 12 will explore what companies from other countries can learn from their Korean rivals. The bottom line of this book is that Tiger Management is indeed sustainable and should therefore be studied seriously by managers of non-Korean firms. A better understanding of Tiger Management will help when competing or collaborating with Korean companies. More generally, given the Korean firms' great success, it is worthwhile to consider what can be learned from them.

Part II

The rise of Korean companies and Tiger Management

2 The seeds of Tiger Management
Foundations of Korean capitalism

My dream is to develop a company and contribute to building national wealth. It is a businessman's social responsibility and obligation to make a company profitable.

Lee Byung-chull, late founder of Samsung Group[1]

Some men live without thinking. Other men with positive thinking achieve ten or one hundred times as much as ordinary people.

Chung Ju-yung, late founder of Hyundai Group[2]

The incentive system is the greatest invention of the century, turning the tide favorably for capitalism.

Lee Kun-hee, Chairman of Samsung Group[3]

Chairmen of Korean business groups and companies are well known for their public statements. Their declarations have an enormous meaning for their companies' employees and for the Korean public in general, as they are powerful and respected leaders of the country's business community. They reveal beliefs and attitudes that sometimes do not look particularly coherent, or are even conflicting on the surface. They expect obedience from the people working for them. At times, they show a caring and communitarian face which seems typical for leaders in collectivistic East Asian countries. At other occasions, they emphasize a Western style focus on individual efforts and performance. In reality, all these facets are complementing each other in the peculiar Korean management style. As will be shown in this chapter, Tiger Management has, in fact, very diverse origins.

Where do Korean capitalism and Tiger Management come from?

In order to understand the origins of Tiger Management, it is necessary to have a look at the roots and the formation process of modern capitalism in Korea as a whole. The contemporary Korean capitalism as well as Korean management has evolved from four origins: traditional Korean culture (in particular, Confucianism), Japanese influence, American influence, and military-led industrialization. The significance of these four forces will be discussed subsequently.

Confucianism

Over its long history, Korea has been influenced in various ways by its big neighbor, China. However, one aspect of Chinese culture and philosophy, which had a particularly strong impact on Korea, is Confucianism. Whereas Confucius lived in China around 500 BC, his thoughts were introduced in Korea about 1,000 years ago and had a shaping influence on Korean society during the long reign of the Yi dynasty, which lasted from 1392 to 1910. During this period, Koreans developed their own interpretation of Confucianism, and, in certain aspects, Confucian thought has been applied in Korea in a stricter way than in China itself. Overall, Korea's society was strongly dominated by Confucianism until the nineteenth century. In fact, Yi dynasty Korea is believed to have been the most ideal Confucian state ever to exist anywhere on earth.[4]

Confucianism emphasizes the strict observance of human relationships in order to maintain order and harmony within a society. In particular, the following "five cardinal relationships" are brought forward:[5]

> The relationship between father and son
> The relationship between monarch and subject
> The relationship between husband and wife
> The relationship between elder brother and younger brother
> The relationship between friend and friend

It is noteworthy that most of these types of relationships are strictly hierarchical in nature: sons have to respect and obey to their fathers, subjects to the monarch, wives to husbands, and younger brothers to elder brothers. Thus, through such Confucian morale a strict hierarchical order is established in a society. Everybody has a well-defined position and has to obey to individuals who are ranked higher.

Furthermore, the importance of one specific dimension of human relationships has been particularly elevated in Korean society through Confucian thought: the relative age of individuals. Koreans became accustomed to building hierarchical relationships based on their age not only within families (between "fathers and sons" or "elder and younger brothers"), but also in all other social relationships. According to this logic, an older person is always in a superior position in a relationship with a younger person who has to pay respect to the former. In return, the older person should help the younger person by guiding and advising him or her.

At the same time, however, an individual's formal rank within organizational hierarchies, such as companies, is also extremely important. In Korean organizations, superiors have a much stronger leverage over their subordinates than in Western countries, as is being reflected in a relatively higher power distance score in cross-cultural studies.[6] Therefore, lower ranked individuals find it very difficult or outright impossible to challenge or defy the orders given to them by their superiors.

Another important aspect of Confucianism is a strong family orientation, as three of the above "five cardinal relationships" are between family members. Koreans are regarded as one of the most family oriented people in the world. In practice, this means that they have a strong tendency to keep fortunes and important assets, including the ownership and managerial control of companies, within their families. Also, family-like relationships are often applied to non-family contexts. For example, the employees of Korean companies often liken their organizations to families in which they are members. They routinely position themselves as elder (or younger) "brothers" or "sisters" of their younger (or elder) colleagues within teams or other organizational units in their firms. The unit's head (and on the company level, the chairman) takes the role of the "father" who has almost unlimited authority over his "family members."[7]

Moreover, although not immediately visible from the "five cardinal relationships," the value of education is also strongly emphasized by Korean-style Confucianism.[8] According to this school of thought, studying is the principle way to qualify for leadership. Virtue and authority are achieved through extensive studies at prestigious educational institutions. Thus, Koreans perceive that a high level of education does not only elevate their social status within society, but also increases their opportunities to pursue a successful professional career. The roots of the Korean education zeal, which is outstanding even by East Asian standards, can be clearly seen here.

One further aspect of Confucian thought that has a particularly strong influence in Korea is "*chung.*" It may be understood as loyalty to the king and the country. As Korea has been repeatedly invaded by foreign military forces throughout its history and great sacrifices were made to maintain national independence, there is a strong common understanding among Koreans that loyalty to their country takes precedence over personal interests. Specifically, during the country's industrialization, this sentiment has motivated Korean managers and workers to make a huge collective effort and work very hard when they were told by their government that this effort is needed to create a strong industrialized nation.[9]

Taken together, Confucianism has not only dominated Korean society for many centuries, but also had a lasting influence on the social behavior of Koreans in various ways. Specifically, social relationships are shaped in a strictly hierarchical manner based on age and position, and family ties and educational merits are strongly emphasized.

Such traditional hierarchical values may appear outdated now in a modern and democratic industrial society. In fact, they have been increasingly challenged in Korea throughout the last decades, as will be discussed in Chapter 11. However, because of their strong and deep cultural roots, they still have considerable effect. Moreover, hierarchical social behavior has been reinforced through an important institution in modern Korea: the country's military. On account of the continued military threat from the North, young Korean males have to complete a long and compulsory military service, with almost no exceptions. Through this service, they get used to taking and executing orders from superiors strictly and unconditionally.[10] It appears, overall, that the military service experience exerts quite a strong influence on the mindset and behavior of the male workforce in Korea regarding hierarchical relationships, much more so than in other countries. Moreover, the influence of the military command culture in Korea has been further amplified by the country's military-led industrialization in the 1960s and 1970s, as will be explained later in this chapter.

Japanese influence

The second important force that shaped the formation of Korean capitalism and management was Japanese influence, which was particularly strong during the first half of the twentieth century. Since the 1870s, an increasing number of Japanese have come to Korea, initially with the primary intention to trade. Subsequently, the economic and political influence of Japanese government officials and merchants in Korea grew steadily stronger and eventually resulted in the country's formal annexation in 1910. Thereafter, Korea remained under Japanese control until the end of the Second World War in 1945.[11]

The domination of Korea by Japan during this period was not a historical coincidence. On the political level, it can be related to the fact that, under the Yi dynasty, the Korean state subjugated itself to a tributary relationship with China from which, in return, it sought protection from intruders. During the late nineteenth and early twentieth century, however, China was too weak to protect Korea from Japanese domination.[12]

At the same time, the growing Japanese influence during this period had a strong economic background. As a result of its long-lasting isolation during the later centuries of the Yi dynasty, Korea was economically and technically backward during this period – not only compared with the rising Western powers, but also with Japan.[13] The Korean landlords could extricate sufficient tributes from the peasants subordinated to them to tribute themselves to the state and thereby maintain their comfortable status. They had no incentive to introduce changes to the status quo, and economic activity was stagnating. Handicraft and manufacturing activities were underdeveloped, and even declining, as luxury goods were mostly imported from China. Above all, merchants had a distinctively low status in the Confucian Korean state, and the elite class of *yangban* (noblemen) which was ruling and administrating the country concentrated its efforts on contemplative scholarship rather than commercial ambitions. In the absence of a modern currency system, barley and rice served as the main mediums of economic exchange.

Given this situation, it is rather unsurprising that Korea was largely defenseless in the late nineteenth century against a Japan which was not only technologically more advanced, but also quickly established many institutions of modern capitalism such as a standardized currency, a modern law system, and a centralized administration. Japan rapidly introduced these institutions after its own opening to foreign trade in 1853 and the Meiji restoration of 1868.[14]

One important aspect of the Japanese influence on the Korean economy and Korean management has been the introduction of basic institutions of capitalism. The Japanese Yen quickly became the dominant currency after Japanese merchants entered Korea. After Japan formally assumed control over Korea in 1910, a large number of reforms were introduced within a few years: the abolition of slavery, the codification of a civil law, the introduction of a tax system based on cash payments, the establishment of a juridical system which was separated from executive powers, and a land reform which incorporated the granting of formal property rights to landlords.[15] Subsequently, the landlords collected rents instead of tributes from the peasants and passed them on to the state.

Moreover, the Japanese rulers also engaged in the creation of a financial and commercial infrastructure (establishing banks, other financial companies, and industrial manufacturing firms in a variety of industries) as well as transportation infrastructure (building a road and railroad system). However, the aforementioned institutional reforms were even more fundamental as they demolished the premodern Confucian state and economic system in a short period of time.

At the same time, the Japanese used their position as colonial rulers to dominate most commercial activity. In particular, the manufacturing sector was mainly controlled by large Japanese business groups (*zaibatsu*). Korean companies were marginalized and could only exceptionally reach a size which allowed them efficient, large-scale industrial production.[16] It was apparently very difficult to run and sustain organized business for Koreans under the harsh Japanese administration. Moreover, in the later years of Japanese colonial rule, many Koreans were, often by force, dislocated either within Korea or to Japan or Manchuria as part of the Japanese war mobilization efforts.[17] This brought not only a lot of hardship on many Koreans, but also meant a radical departure from the previously stable situation where families typically resided in the same location for many generations.

Thus, in stark contrast to the past, Koreans were suddenly given incentives to start up commercial activities both in a positive and in a negative sense. In the positive sense, the fundamental motivation for any modern business activity, the accumulation of capital and wealth, was now being provided and Koreans were also given opportunities to study modern management systems by observing the activities of Japanese companies. In fact, the centralized and diversified business structure of the *zaibatsu* was emulated by many Korean entrepreneurs in the decades after liberation from Japan.[18] In the negative sense, many Koreans may have seen no other choice to survive than engaging in business activities, often under very adverse conditions and against all odds. This implanted a strong survival instinct as well as the tendency to conduct bold, risky strategies among Korean entrepreneurs. They often had little or nothing to lose.

Taken together, the Japanese influenced the Korean economy as well as the management of Korean firms in various important ways. First, they laid the foundation for the development of modern capitalism in Korea through successive economic reforms. In particular, through the establishment of property rights and a modern law system, Koreans were now given incentives to start business activities as they could retain and accumulate capital. Second, through the establishment of a centralized state bureaucracy and the activities of large Japanese firms, role models for operating and managing modern, capitalist enterprises were provided. Third, through a harsh colonial rule that resulted in deterioration of living standards and through the dislocation of many individuals which pulled them out of the relative comfort of their home towns or villages, Koreans were often induced to start up business activities out of sheer survival necessities.

American influence

The third important force that shaped the management system of Korean firms was influence from the United States of America. The significance of this influence mainly stems from the dominant presence of the US military on the Southern half of the Korean peninsula during the first decades after liberation from Japanese occupation.

In the years after 1945, Korea was effectively divided into two parts: the Southern half came under American influence and the Northern half under Soviet influence. After the declaration of an independent state (the Republic of Korea) in the South in 1948, American troops retreated from Korea, only to re-enter soon thereafter in an emergency operation by leading UN forces to rescue the South Korean state which was invaded by the North in June 1950. The Korean War eventually ended in an armistice in 1953, and the US military kept a big presence in the South thereafter.

The American presence in Korea has not been restricted to a military role, however. American officials played a decisive role in keeping the public order after the withdrawal of the Japanese in 1945, in helping to establish the South Korean state, and in giving reconstruction aid as well as general development aid during and after the Korean War.

On the administrative level, one important reform carried out under American guidance was a second land reform in which land was redistributed from land-owners to peasants.[19] It was considered a success, as the agricultural production could be greatly increased, and idle capital was turned away from land speculation and directed towards manufacturing. Also through this reform, the ancient feudal *yangban* class was dismantled; further preparing the ground for modern capitalism and competition based on capabilities not class affiliations.

Reconstruction and development aid also played an important role in the American influence on Korea's economy. Its scale was immense: it amounted, even excluding military spending, to about fifteen percent of Korean GDP (gross domestic product) in the 1950s.[20] Moreover, the way it was spent and distributed also exerted a major influence not only on the Korean economy as a whole, but also on the management of Korean firms. Most aid was administered by the Korean government and given to companies in the form of (often non-repayable) loans, allocation of hard currency for importing raw materials, tax exemptions, and preferential contracts for governmental infrastructure projects.

It appears that these favors to specific companies were often given based on personal networks or corruption of government officials. All the same, they allowed many Korean firms to grow quickly.[21] Moreover, as most of the preferential treatment was not industry-specific or focused on the import of raw materials, Korean entrepreneurs and managers were induced to seize whatever business opportunity was given to them, thereby laying the ground for the aggressive diversification strategies Korean firms became famous for later on.

The American influence on Korean management has also been exerted in more indirect ways, however. Through their strong presence in Korea and the close military, political, and economic ties between the two countries, the US became a benchmark for professional management as well as a preferred destination for many Koreans to study and work. As these professionals often eventually return to Korea and apply the management knowledge and practice they have acquired in the US at home, the American mindset to compete based on capabilities and to strive for high efficiency and effectiveness has been steadily permeating into the management of Korean firms throughout the last decades.

Taken together, the management of Korean firms has been influenced by the US in various ways. Through institutional reforms (particularly, the land reform), Koreans were provided with a more equal playing field to compete based on their capabilities and skills. The striving for performance has been reinforced during the last decades by the steady flow of Korean students and professionals to the US and then back to Korea. Moreover, through the significant reconstruction and development aid provided by the US during and after the Korean War, many Korean firms were given good initial growth opportunities. Through the way the programs have been implemented, Korean entrepreneurs have become accustomed to think big and to seize growth opportunities across industries.

Military-led industrialization

The fourth and final underlying force that shaped Tiger Management was the strong military influence on Korea's economic development in the 1960s and 1970s. In the first thirteen years after its establishment, Korea was governed by civilian administrations that proved largely incapable of elevating the country's level of economic development. The desperate economic situation and widespread political unrest then induced Major General Park Chung-hee, together with a group of military officers, to seize power in a coup in May 1961. Thereafter, Park became president and ruled the country until 1979, when he was assassinated.[22]

The new government radically changed policies and launched a series of five-year economic plans. The country's economic development became the top governmental priority. In the first two plans, which covered the periods from 1962–66 and 1967–71, the growth of export-oriented manufacturing industries was strongly emphasized.[23] Regarding its goals, the Park administration's economic policies had therefore some similarities with the Japanese "developmental state" that also relied on discretionary government intervention and planning to promote industrialization.[24]

In contrast to postwar Japan, however, economic planning was implemented in a military command style in the Korea of the 1960s and 1970s.[25] The five-year plans laid down specific development targets and were broken down into annual economic management plans which contained even more concrete goals. At the same time, the government maximized its control over the economy. Banks were nationalized, and an Economic Planning Board was created. This Board supervised the implementation of the development plans and had strong discretionary power over the government bureaucracy as well as the private sector. In order to realize the government's development targets, specific companies were selected and "ordered" to invest into specific industries and activities.

As a result, this top-down military command culture subsequently permeated into the corporate sector. Business leaders were at a pinch to meet the government's targets according to the given timelines, and tended to pass on this pressure to their subordinates in a similar manner. Managers and workers got used to working very hard and under strong time pressure.

The period of intense military-led industrialization therefore had a strong impact on the management of Korean firms in several ways. Business plans were developed and handed down in a top-down command style. Moreover, the targets contained in these plans were typically clear cut and linked to specific and ambitious time lines. Therefore, companies learned to work on specific targets and implement business plans with very high speed. They became so accustomed to high-speed implementation that the word "*palli palli*" (quickly quickly) became customary in conversations among managers and workers. Furthermore, as the government accepted no failures and excuses in its economic development drive, corporate leaders also tended to adopt a similar attitude and imposed a strong performance pressure on their subordinates. Everybody got used to working very hard and to doing whatever was needed to meet business targets.

Summary: the seeds of Tiger Management

As the previous discussion has shown, Confucianism, Japanese influence, American influence, and military-led industrialization have all had a strong and lasting effect, not only on Korean society and its economy, but also on the way Korean companies are managed and operated. The main related points are summarized in Table 2.1.

Table 2.1 The seeds of Tiger Management

Confucianism	Japanese influence	American influence	Military-led industrialization
Hierarchical social relationships based on age and status	Centrally controlled diversified business structure	Competition orientation	Military command culture
Emphasis on family relationships	Accumulating capital based on diligence	Professional pragmatism	Working on clear-cut targets
Strong emphasis on educational merits	Sustaining under difficult conditions	Seizing opportunities	Quick execution of plans
Strong national loyalty	Geographic mobility	Global mindset	No tolerance of failure

As can be seen, these four forces shaped the management of Korean firms in very distinctive ways, and some of their effects appear to be conflicting and countervailing. For example, the Confucian concept of strong and unquestioned hierarchy appears to be directly opposed to US style pragmatism and competition orientation. However, as will be shown in the following chapters, Korean companies created a unique management blend from these influences that is labeled Tiger Management in this book. They managed to combine different parts from the four foundations in ways that complemented each other rather than creating unproductive conflicts. Thereby, Korean companies eventually became the strong and formidable competitors they are nowadays – first in their home country, then internationally. This genesis and evolution of Tiger Management will be discussed in the following chapters.

3 Rising Tigers

The early growth stages

> We succeeded because our people devoted their enterprising spirits. They used the force of their minds. Conviction creates indomitable efforts. This is the key to miracles. Man's potential is limitless.
>
> Chung Ju-yung[1]

For most of its history, Korea has been regarded by Westerners as a mostly irrelevant North-East Asian backwater on the global political and economic landscape. After 1945, the country was in the headlines as the place where a devastating war was fought. This war involved not only the two Korean states, but also the US and other Western powers, which backed the South, and communist China, which backed the North. Observers also took notice of the country's sorry state of economic development and the bitter poverty under which its population had to live. What went unnoticed for many years was the deep transformation from a feudal agricultural to a modern industrial society that has been ongoing in Korea since the early twentieth century. What few people realized also was the dramatic growth and success of Korean companies. Korean entrepreneurs, eventually being allowed to make full use of their talents in a market economy, converted a war-torn country with little infrastructure into an industrial powerhouse within just a few decades. They employed managerial methods and strategies previously unheard of. Unnoticed by the world, Tiger Management was born.

Humble beginnings: early Korean entrepreneurs

As the feudal Korean economy of the Yi dynasty was centered on agriculture and on the needs of the royal court and the ruling *yangban* class, capitalist entrepreneurship did not develop on any significant scale. The ruling aristocrats could satisfy their needs for manufactured and handicraft goods through the exchange of tributes with Chinese courts and the supplies provided by government owned factories. As a result, there was not much demand for goods produced by private domestic industries. Early efforts by the Korean government to set up a few model factories with modern equipment appear to have been largely ineffective because of the absence of a stable financial system that could supply working capital and a lack of skilled managers and entrepreneurs.[2] According to official statistics, in 1903 there existed only six factories in the whole country under domestic ownership with a total workforce of ninety-two employees.[3]

After the Japanese annexation of Korea in 1910, however, the situation changed drastically. The Japanese rulers introduced basic institutions of modern capitalism such as a civil law code, property rights, and a taxation system. The pre-modern Korean society was effectively dismantled within a short period of time. In this sense, important foundations for the development of entrepreneurial activity were laid, as assets could now be acquired and capital could be accumulated more systematically.[4]

At the same time, however, new hurdles were created for Koreans to engage in entrepreneurial activity. Until around 1920, the formation of companies was subject to official approval, and few such approvals were given to Koreans. Even thereafter, only small-scale industries were regarded as "desirable" to be owned and operated by Korean nationals.[5] Large-scale manufacturing, in contrast, was dominated by Japanese business groups (*zaibatsu*). As a result, most newly established factories were owned and managed by Japanese nationals. In these Japanese owned companies, Koreans were mostly confined to the positions of workers and lower level managers. They were given little opportunity to gain experience at senior management levels.[6]

Notwithstanding these formidable obstacles, however, a new class of Korean entrepreneurs gradually emerged during the period of Japanese occupation. After 1919, some of them could take advantage of the somewhat friendlier policies by the Japanese colonial administration. When being confronted with the Korean independence movement, the Japanese deemed the collaboration with some influential Koreans as important to sustain their rule. Supported financially by state-affiliated institutions, a few Korean businessmen subsequently managed to create medium-sized company groups, such as those built around the Tongil Bank, the Whashin Department Stores, and the Kyongsong Textile Company.[7]

There can be no doubt that in Korea the business sector during the period of Japanese occupation was dominated by companies owned and managed by Japanese nationals. In 1944, Japanese owned companies accounted for no less than 92 percent of the incorporated industrial companies in Korea and for 97.1 percent of their paid-up capital.[8] From this point of view, it appears that little Korean entrepreneurship could develop during this time span.

From a developmental perspective, however, the picture looks rather different. In 1939, there were 4,185 Korean owned industrial factories counted,[9] a huge increase when compared with only six of them in 1903. In other words, notwithstanding Japanese occupation and colonization, quite a considerable domestically owned industrial base developed in Korea in a rather short period of time out of almost nothing.

Descriptions of Korean businessmen during this period reveal that many of them originated from poor families, did not receive any formal education, and started their companies with very little capital which was privately raised such as by selling their families' house or by saving money earned as employees of other companies.[10] They learned from and imitated production processes introduced by Japanese factories in Korea as well as in mainland Japan. Steadily threatened by Japanese and domestic competition, they mostly survived by means of sheer will power and perseverance.

At the same time, an early Korean business elite emerged.[11] Business people like Park Hung-sik, who established various trading and retailing companies under the brand name Whashin, and Kim Song-su, who founded the Kyongsong Textile Company, were prominent representatives of this small class of larger scale entrepreneurs. Whereas Park received an elementary school education, Kim graduated from Waseda University in political science. Aside from their somewhat higher education level and wealthier family backgrounds, these entrepreneurs developed their businesses partially by the same virtues as their smaller scale peers at the time: thriftiness and strong perseverance in an adverse environment. Additionally, they managed to build good relations with the Japanese colonial authorities that enabled them to gain access to governmental loans and to larger scale business opportunities – for example by becoming subcontractors for Japanese companies. In other words, they developed not only basic business process skills, but also skills of relationship building with the colonial authorities and Japanese companies. They strengthened their companies' competitiveness further through systematic employee training programs. Some of them even showed a commitment to enter foreign markets such as China, Manchuria, or the Philippines.

Taken together, the first generation of Korean entrepreneurs already accomplished remarkable achievements in a harsh environment under Japanese colonial rule. Being given the basic opportunity to create and run capitalist private businesses, they created many small scale and a few larger companies in a wide range of industries including manufacturing, trading, and retailing. Some important elements of Tiger Management were already visible at that time: a strong entrepreneurial mindset that always searches for new business opportunities and an ability to endure under difficult conditions.

Post-liberation emergence and growth (1945–60)

After the Japanese occupation forces left Korea in 1945, it might have been expected that the country would experience an economic boom. Massive restrictions and discriminations that Korean businesses had to endure as a result of Japanese colonization and, since the late 1930s, widespread military hostilities when East Asia became a battlefield of the Second World War suddenly came to an end.

However, it was the total reverse of such a post-occupation and post-war boom that actually happened to Korea in the first decade after 1945. In fact, the country experienced a period of chaos, economic depression, and devastation. There were two reasons for this. First, the Japanese colonial administration left a huge institutional void behind when it dissolved itself. There was no organized transition and handover of control from the Japanese to the Koreans. Moreover, the Koreans were not prepared to take over their own country as the pre-modern administrative structure has been demolished by the Japanese and the Koreans had no experience of running a modern state and economy. Therefore, the first post-war years were chaotic, resulting in a serious depression of economic activity. Industrial production in 1948 amounted only to 14 percent of the level reached in 1938.[12]

Second, Korea was victimized by the cold war. After 1945, the country was effectively divided into a southern part, which came under American influence, and a northern part, which came under Soviet and, later on, Chinese influence. As a result, two different Korean states were created in 1948: the Republic of Korea in the South and the Democratic People's Republic of Korea in the North. As the Northern state was built on a communist ideology and economic system, entrepreneurial activity could only be continued in the South – the part of the country that was relatively less industrialized. To make things worse, the Korean War, which had broken out between the two states in 1950 and lasted until 1953, destroyed large parts of the economic and industrial infrastructure left behind by the Japanese.

Notwithstanding all this turmoil and war related destruction, the period after 1945 also provided South Korean businesses with new opportunities, however. One such opportunity was the access to formerly Japanese industrial assets left behind in Korea. These assets accounted for thirty percent of the country's economy, and were initially nationalized after liberation. Most of them, however, were subsequently sold to private individuals or companies based on personal networks and preferences and not via public auctions. Importantly, the former Japanese businesses were sold at book values. Owing to high inflation in the post-liberation period, these book values amounted to only a fraction of their fair market values.

Moreover, only a small part of the total price had to be transferred at the time of the purchase while the remaining balance could be paid down over fifteen years without any interest payment.[13] Taken together, the re-privatization of nationalized assets taken over from the Japanese created a golden opportunity for many Korean companies to expand the scale and scope of their operations.

Another important factor that created new opportunities for business growth in Korea was the reconstruction aid given by the US in the years during and after the Korean War. From 1953 to 1958, this aid amounted to no less than fifteen percent of Korea's GDP and eighty percent of the country's foreign exchange. A significant part of this aid was used by the Korean government to establish an import substitution policy. Hard foreign currency was allocated to companies that imported raw materials and processed these materials into final products. This allocation of import quotas and of foreign exchange to buy raw materials from abroad was hugely attractive for Korean companies for various reasons. First, there was a dual exchange rate of the Korean Won, and the exchange rate applied for the import of raw materials was much more favorable than the official exchange rate.[14] Second, as the Korean market in these sectors was shielded from foreign competition, final products could be sold at relatively high prices to Korean consumers.

The development aid received by the US was also distributed to the business sector in various other ways. Companies could receive non-repayable loans at subsidized (in real terms: negative) interest rates. They were also exempted from taxation. Finally, some companies were given huge business opportunities through preferential contracts for large-scale government projects that were carried out to rebuild the country's infrastructure.[15]

A major problem with all these business support policies in the 1950s was their unevenness and lack of transparency. Instead of being publicly announced and auctioned, loans, tax breaks, hard currency, and government contracts were given by government officials to those business people they were acquainted with – often in return for personal favors. It is also disputable whether the import substitution policy of this period was well designed to accelerate the country's economic development. The easiest way to turn import quotas into profits was to take advantage of the differential between the official and the preferred exchange rate of the Won. As a result, many companies focused on low value added activities, such as sugar refining, flour milling, or cotton weaving (labeled as the "three white industries") where the cost of raw materials amounted to more than eighty percent of the total cost of the final product.[16] In other words, the incentive structure of the import substitution policies was skewed towards light industries. Aside from these incentive effects and the inevitable focus on construction when rebuilding the country's infrastructure, however, the governmental support policies were not targeted at specific sectors. As a result, companies that could get access to government aid could often use it for *any* business activity that looked promising at that time.[17] This non-specific nature of governmental support nurtured a growth-oriented mentality of Korean entrepreneurs who tended to jump on any emerging business opportunity even when this implied a venture into unrelated industries, as the risk was strongly mitigated by the various support schemes. After having endured a very restrictive business environment during the colonial period, Korean companies and their owners now learned to pursue aggressive growth and diversification strategies.

In sum, notwithstanding all the post-liberation chaos and wartime devastation, the period after 1945 provided huge growth opportunities to those Korean businesspeople that had access to, and the favor of, government officials. First, they could pick up formerly Japanese assets for relatively little money. Second, they could extend the size and scope of their business by taking advantage of various governmental support schemes. As a result, diversified business groups (*chaebols*) of quite considerable size emerged for the first time. In fact, the majority of *chaebols*, which dominated the Korean economy in the following decades, were founded in the period between 1945 and 1960.[18] Most of the leading *chaebols* of that time were engaged in international trade (mainly, the importation of raw materials) as well as manufacturing, mainly in light industries, and various services such as banking, securities, or insurance.[19]

The boom years of the 1960s and 1970s

In the early 1960s, the business environment in Korea again changed drastically as a result of political events. In April 1960, popular unrest over widespread corruption and a disputed election resulted in the downfall of the government of President Rhee Syngman who had ruled the country since its foundation in 1948. Thereafter, there was a brief period of democratic government and continued unrest, which abruptly ended in a military coup in May 1961 by Park Chung-hee. President Park, born during Japanese occupation into a poor family in Gyeongnam province, became an officer in the Imperial Japanese army and served during the final stage of World War Two in Manchuria. Later on, he joined the Korean army and quickly moved up in its ranks.

As mentioned in Chapter 2, the new government introduced new policies and launched a series of five-year economic plans. Initially, the change of government spelled trouble for *chaebol* owners who had thrived during the Rhee regime. Many of them were arrested and indicted based on corruption charges related to bribes they had paid to officials of the former government in exchange for receiving access to import quotas and other governmental aid. However, most of them were released soon after promising to collaborate with the new government as officials realized that they needed the business leaders to achieve their development goals.[20]

Under the Park regime, a strong authoritarian state was created to lead economic development through an export promotion policy. Specific business groups were selected for large-scale investments in those industries regarded as "strategic." In the 1960s, these industries were mainly labor intensive light industries, such as textiles or clothing, and capital intensive basic industries, such as oil refining or cement. In the 1970s, the focus shifted to heavy industries and assembly industries, including steel, petrochemicals, non-ferrous metals, machinery, shipbuilding, and electronics. Mostly, only two or three business groups were selected to lead the development in each designated industry. These selected companies were then supported through a variety of measures that were partially similar to those existing in the 1950s: low interest loans provided by government controlled financial institutions, tax credits, preferential tariffs, and an effective shielding of the Korean market from competition by other companies, thereby giving incumbents an opportunity to gain monopolistic profits.[21] Moreover, when some leading companies faced bankruptcy during the oil crises of the 1970s, the government bailed them out by writing off loans and providing fresh capital.[22]

Therefore, similarly to the 1950s, the growth and profitability of *chaebols* throughout the 1960s and 1970s was strongly determined by their relations to the Korean government. Nonetheless, business-government relations changed fundamentally between the two periods.[23] Whereas their nature was collusive and based on personal ties of business leaders to key government officials in the 1950s, the government clearly took the lead in the 1960s and 1970s by selecting specific companies to invest in specific industries. Also, as the selection of companies for investment projects now became the result of a systematic, top-down economic planning process, the perceived competence of companies to conduct these projects successfully became a more important selection criteria as compared to the strength of personal ties with officials. Consequently, the ranks of leading *chaebols* drastically changed between the two periods. Whereas some of the champions from the 1950s fell out of the group of leading companies, others continued to thrive together with a number of newcomers.[24]

In contrast to the first years after the Korean War, the country's economic development was hugely successful during the 1960s and 1970s. Annual economic growth averaged almost eight percent during these two decades and exceeded ten percent in many single years. Per capita income increased from US$79 in 1960 to US$1,597 in 1980.[25] Consequently, Korean companies also grew rapidly, particularly those favored by the government. Their revenues often increased by more than fifty percent on an annual basis.

It could be argued that these Korean companies and their leaders had an "easy time" throughout the whole period from 1945 to the 1970s, as they could first take advantage of personal favors given by government officials and later followed the government's lead and received its full support when unfolding their investment plans. External factors also contributed to Korea's economic development. The country received significant financial and technological aid from the US, and later on from Japan after the two countries resumed diplomatic ties in 1965. Moreover, the fast development of manufacturing industries was further supported by the high education and skill level of the Korean population, which exceeded by far that of other similarly poor countries and strongly reflected Confucian cultural traditions.

Notwithstanding all these favorable circumstances, however, the transformation of the *chaebols* from the obscure conglomerates of the 1950s, that were mostly centered on importing raw materials and low value added manufacturing, to the diversified business empires of the 1970s was neither "simple" nor "inevitable." Instead, it required the bold entrepreneurship of business leaders to achieve such a massive growth and transformation. With hindsight, it is easy to say that the groups just followed the government's lead and relied on its support. In reality, it must have been extremely challenging to continuously advance into ever new industries and set up ever new operations with limited experience and resources. Also, Korea was a developing country at that time with a patchy infrastructure at best, further adding to the difficulties of running large and diversified business groups.

The interplay between the government's strong guidance and support, its rapidly changing priorities in terms of industrial sectors to be developed, and the *chaebol* leaders' relentless expansion efforts also lastingly forged the structure of the business groups in several important ways. First, the groups became extremely diversified, as they extended their activities into ever new industries. Second, as the *chaebols* could receive cheap loans, they preferred debt over equity financing when growing their businesses, resulting in an increase of their debt/equity ratios from around 100 percent in the early 1960s to 400 percent and more in the 1970s,[26] Third, the government (and consequently, the business groups) focused on the establishment of final assembly operations in a wide range of sectors but did not make similarly intensive efforts to nurture supporting industries, and many parts and intermediate goods had to be imported because of a lack of domestic suppliers. As a result, Korean manufacturing companies became less vertically integrated than their counterparts in most other countries. Finally, as the Park government nationalized banks after 1961, the *chaebols* mostly centered their activities on manufacturing and international trade.

The five largest business groups

The five largest Korean business groups are briefly introduced here to illustrate their formation, growth, and transformation until the 1970s. These examples show that it was in this period of Korea's rise from a neglected backwater to an industrial powerhouse in East Asia when Tiger Management first fully emerged. Key data regarding the overall development of the groups between 1960 and 2010 are summarized in Tables 3.1 to 3.5.

Samsung Group[27]

Samsung Group, which is currently the largest *chaebol*, is also the oldest one among the five biggest Korean business groups. It was founded by Lee Byung-chull, who was born in 1911 the younger son of a wealthy farmer in Kyongnam Province. In 1938, Lee established a trading company that mainly exported agricultural products. After liberation, the focus shifted to importing basic goods that were not available in Korea.

Samsung's business first took off in the 1950s. A sugar manufacturing company (Cheil Jedang) was established in 1953 and a textile factory (Cheil Industries) in 1954. His close relationship with President Rhee Syngman helped Chairman Lee to secure the foreign currency needed to import the facilities for his factories. Moreover, after Samsung had started its production of sugar and of woolen textiles, the government banned imports of these goods and thereby effectively gave Samsung monopolies in the Korean market. With the profits from these businesses, the group acquired an insurance company and several banks.

At the beginning of President Park Chung-hee's regime, Samsung faced many difficulties because of the group's close relationship with the previous Rhee government. Chairman Lee was initially charged with corruption, but then managed to repair his relationship with President Park by calling for support for the new government in the Korean business community and handing over the group's financial service companies as well as a newly built fertilizer manufacturing facility to the government.

In the late 1960s and throughout the 1970s, Samsung then diversified its business again, mainly into "strategic sectors" identified by the government, such as electronics, petrochemicals, machinery, and shipbuilding. At the same time, the group made efforts to integrate vertically its manufacturing operations through investments into the electrical parts and glass industries.

The most important venture Samsung made in this period was into the electronics industry. In 1969, Samsung Electronics was founded together with a joint venture with Japan's Sanyo, and the assembly of TVs and radios was started.

Table 3.1 Key data on the development of Samsung Group

Indicator	1960	1970	1980	1990	2000	2010
Number of group companies	3	12	22	30	45	71
Main industries	Trade, finance, sugar	Trade, finance, sugar, fertilizer, newspaper, electronics	Trade, finance, sugar, fertilizer, electronics, shipbuilding	Trade, finance, electronics, shipbuilding chemicals	Finance, insurance, electronics, shipbuilding, fashion, hotel, construction	Finance, insurance, electronics, shipbuilding, fashion, hotel, construction
Number of employees	1,871	9,080	75,000	178,520	110,018	275,000
Sales (in billion KRW)	2.7	36.5	2,385.5	29,281.8	101,241	220,120

Source: Korea Fair Trade Commission, *Companies affiliated with large business groups*; Samsung Group homepage; journal and newspaper articles.

Table 3.2 Key data on the development of Hyundai Group

Indicator	1960	1970	1980	1990	2000	2010[d]
Number of group companies	1	6[b]	31	39	35	43
Main industries	Construction	Construction, automobiles, shipbuilding	Construction, automobiles, shipbuilding	Construction, automobiles, shipbuilding	Construction, automobiles, shipbuilding, finance	Automobiles, steel, finance, logistics, construction, resorts
Number of employees	125	n/a	156,000[c]	167,000	180,000	120,000
Sales (in billion KRW)	0.36[a]	25.1	2,880.3	22,658	95,047	94,652

Source: Korea Fair Trade Commission, *Companies affiliated with large business groups*; journal and newspaper articles.

Notes: (a) 1961; (b) 1972; (c) 1985; (d) data for 2010 refer to Hyundai Motor Group, largest successor of Hyundai Group, which broke up in 2000.

Table 3.3 Key data on the development of LG Group

Indicator	1960	1970	1980	1990	2000	2010
Number of group companies	4	8	14	20	43	60
Main industries	Trade, electronics, chemicals	Trade, electronics, chemicals	Trade, electronics, chemicals, oil refining	Electronics, chemicals, oil refining, communication networks	Electronics, chemicals, oil refining, communication networks, construction	Electronics, chemicals, communication networks, fashion
Number of employees	660[a]	n/a	53,000[c]	100,000	81,687	100,000
Sales (in billion KRW)	0.74[b]	52.0	2,700	16,199	59,503	94,638

Source: Korea Fair Trade Commission, *Companies affiliated with large business groups*; journal and newspaper articles.

Note: (a) end of 1950s; (b) 1964; (c) 1979.

Table 3.4 Key data on the development of SK Group

Indicator	1960	1970	1980	1990	2000	2010
Number of group companies	1	5[a]	14	24	39	84
Main industries	Textile	Textile, oil refining, hotel	Textile, oil refining, hotel	Textile, oil refining, gas, hotel, communication networks	Oil refining, gas, communication networks, construction	Oil refining, gas, communication networks, construction, finance
Number of employees	423	2,328	13,916	22,857[c]	19,566	32,000
Sales (in billion KRW)	n/a	89.1[b]	3,074.7	7,611.3	35,735	95,118

Source: Korea Fair Trade Commission, *Companies affiliated with large business groups*; journal and newspaper articles.

Note: (a) 1972; (b) 1975; (c) 1992.

Table 3.5 Key data on the development of Daewoo Group

Indicator	1967	1970	1980	1990	1996
Number of group companies	1	1	32	23	25
Main industries	Trade, textile	Trade, textile	Trade, investment, electronics, shipbuilding, automobiles, construction	Investment, electronics, shipbuilding, automobiles, construction	Electronics, shipbuilding, automobiles, construction
Number of employees	30	700	52,988	85,831	86,314
Sales (in billion KRW)	0.2	2.7	1,871.5	15,759.4	52,439.5

Source: Korea Fair Trade Commission, *Companies affiliated with large business groups*; journal and newspaper articles.

Note: Daewoo Group was founded in 1967 and went bankrupt in 1999.

A few years later, the group established various additional companies related to the electronics business and ventured into the microelectronics industry by taking over Korea Semiconductor Corp. (which was initially a government owned company) in 1977. It should be noted that by global standards, Samsung was still a business group of modest size and had no experience in electronics manufacturing or any related industry whatsoever when it entered this sector and devoted a large part of its financial and human resources in the following years to develop the business. Notwithstanding the governmental support, it was by any standard an extremely bold strategic decision by Chairman Lee to invest into this industry.

Hyundai Group[28]

Hyundai Group was created by Chung Ju-yung, the son of a poor farmer. Chung first became a rice merchant in Seoul in the 1930s and, after being forced out of this business by the Japanese administration, started a car repair shop which he eventually also had to hand over as a result of Japanese war mobilization efforts. After liberation, he re-entered the car repair business and founded Hyundai Auto Service in 1946, followed by a civil engineering company in 1947. Subsequently, the two companies were merged into Hyundai Construction Company in 1950.

Hyundai's business thrived throughout the 1950s as the company conducted construction projects for the US military and the Korean government. It soon established a reputation as the country's leading company in the construction and infrastructure business.

The group continued to grow rapidly in the 1960s by executing President Park's economic development plans. It played a leading role in building Korea's first highway from Seoul to Busan as well as numerous dams and bridges. Thereby, it became the country's largest business group during this period – a position it kept for several decades thereafter.

From the late 1960s Hyundai diversified into other industries. In 1967, Hyundai Motor Corporation, Korea's first automobile manufacturer, was established. In 1973, a shipbuilding company was founded. The group also pursued vertical integration into upstream industries such as cement, concrete, tiles, furniture, electric machinery, and car and ship components throughout the 1970s.

The venture into automobile manufacturing was a particularly entrepreneurial one. Although the founder ran a car repair shop earlier in his career, the group focused on the construction business in the following decades – a field which is technologically and managerially unrelated to the automobile industry. Considering the complexity and high capital and knowledge intensity of automobile manufacturing, entering this sector was very bold and risky for Hyundai at that time.

Another feature Hyundai become famous for was its speed of project execution and business development. For example, it started assembling ships when its new shipyard itself was still under construction.[29]

LG Group[30]

LG Group was founded by Koo In-hwoi, who was born in a relatively wealthy farm village in the southeastern part of Korea. He first operated a retailing and then a trading company in the city of Shinju from the 1930s. Soon after liberation, he scaled up his business and started manufacturing cosmetic articles and soap from 1947 in Busan. Thereafter, a plastics factory was built in order to vertically integrate into soap containers and tooth brushes. As there were no other domestic producers of such articles at that time, and the Rhee government pursued an import substitution policy, the group could establish a monopoly in the Korean market.

The next diversification step was into consumer electronics, which LG entered in 1958 and thereby pioneered that market as the first domestic producer. Supported by the government's economic development plans, the group further diversified into petroleum processing, communication equipment, electronic wires, and insurance throughout the 1960s. The newly added businesses tended to augment existing ones. For example, the insurance business was entered in order to reduce insurance premiums, as a large amount of crude oil needed to be shipped to the petroleum processing plants and the Korean market for marine insurance was underdeveloped.

The group diversified and grew further in the 1970s, mainly into machinery, instruments, and chemicals. Eventually a general trading company was also established.

LG considered synergies with its existing operations more so than other groups when entering new industries. However, many of its strategic decisions were nonetheless highly entrepreneurial and risky. In particular, entering the consumer electronics industry was something unheard of for a modest conglomerate with limited resources, which had its base in a developing country with an income level lower than many African countries at the time.

SK Group[31]

Chey Jong-kun, born in 1926 in Suwon as the eldest son of a wealthy farmer, was the founder of SK Group. He studied at a technical school in Seoul and then became a technician at a textile plant in Suwon, which was owned and operated by the Japanese. After liberation in 1945, the factory became the Korean government's property and was destroyed later on during the Korean War. In 1953, Chey purchased the company from the government, rebuilt the facilities, and reopened the business under its previous name, Sunkyung Weaving Company.

Sunkyung Weaving soon became a leading Korean textile exporter and thereby grew very quickly. From the 1960s, the group rapidly advanced into other industries and participated in the economic development plans of the Park government with which it had good relations. A trading company was founded in 1962, a chemical company in 1969, and a construction company in 1976.

Notwithstanding all these diversification moves, SK Group expanded less aggressively during the 1960s and 1970s when compared with other *chaebols*. In fact, the textile company was in serious financial trouble in the early 1960s, necessitating a strengthening of the core business through the development of new products. However, a big moment came in 1980 when SK acquired Yukong, a state owned oil refinery with revenues that were more than five times larger than SK's. The acquisition was heavily supported by the government. Regardless of the government's help, however, it was still a daring move to take over and integrate a company that was so much larger and that was engaged in a totally different industry. Through the successful integration of Yukong, SK entered the ranks of the leading *chaebols*.

Daewoo Group[32]

Daewoo Group has been the youngest and the most rapidly growing group among the leading Korean *chaebols*. It was founded in 1967 by Kim Woo-choong, a businessman with a university education who started Daewoo as a textile manufacturing and export business. The company grew so rapidly that it accounted for forty percent of Korea's textile exports as soon as 1972. It had a close relationship with the government, which gave it access to export financing at preferential interest rates as well as various other subsidies.

With the profits from the textile business, Daewoo soon advanced into other industries. It ventured into overseas construction projects and established a general trading company.

In contrast to most other Korean business groups, Daewoo further accelerated its growth by taking over other companies that were often insolvent or financially troubled. In 1976, it acquired Hankook Machinery and in 1978 Okpo Shipyard and Saehan Motors. In other words, the group diversified into the machinery, shipbuilding, and automobile industries within just a few years. The government appreciated Daewoo's efforts to save troubled companies and supported it with various subsidies to reorganize these businesses.

Daewoo's growth strategy has been commonly perceived as the most aggressive one among the large *chaebols*. The group continuously used its cash and other resources to undertake ever new (and often unrelated) acquisitions. It also took on the daunting task to turn around and integrate failing companies in various industries. Whereas the Korean government certainly helped Daewoo during these acquisitions, it was still a series of extremely bold and entrepreneurial moves that Chairman Kim conducted.

Synthesis: the emergence of Tiger companies and Tiger Management

The review of the foundation and early growth stages of Korean companies and business groups in this chapter has highlighted a number of environmental factors and managerial features which enabled them to grow big in a short period of time.

The transformation from a pre-modern feudal to a modern capitalist economy, which started during the Japanese occupation in the first half of the twentieth century, first enabled Korean business people to establish and operate companies. At the same time, the Japanese colonial administration's policies severely restricted these activities and created a very difficult environment for Korean businesses. The two common experiences that Korean entrepreneurs came across during this period were (1) that it needs a lot of hard work and perseverance to succeed in business and (2) that good relations with the government are an important factor to secure vital resources and take advantage of growth opportunities.

After 1945, they swiftly capitalized on these experiences by taking full advantage of new opportunities that arose because of the sell-off of former Japanese assets and various support policies of the Korean government. It is important to note that this support for private business was not universal, but was instead concentrated on a limited number of companies favored by government officials. At the same time, the survival skills the Korean entrepreneurs had acquired during the period of Japanese colonization helped them to endure the economic turmoil during the periods of post-liberation chaos and the Korean War.

There are some further interrelated points that successful Korean entrepreneurs had in common during the decades after 1945. First, they were very agile in seizing on any business opportunity that was given to them, particularly through government policies during the post-liberation decades. Though many of them tried to focus on related industries in their diversification efforts, they sometimes also ventured into unrelated fields when the business opportunity looked very promising. Second, they were fundamentally very aggressive and growth oriented in their business strategies and therefore re-invested their profits in order to expand their operations. Third, they swiftly transferred knowledge, re-allocated human and financial resources between their different business activities, and thereby enabled the very quick growth of their business groups. Whenever a new business opportunity – such as a new industry to invest into – arose, all available managers and experts with strong skills and capabilities as well as all available financial resources were shifted to the new field to exploit this opportunity.[33]

Notwithstanding all the government support which some *chaebols* could obtain during this period, their rapid growth and expansion was no small achievement, particularly when keeping in mind that they started as small or tiny companies which commanded very limited human and financial resources, and their leaders had no experience with managing larger companies. It is also noteworthy that only about half of the Korean business leaders who created the *chaebols* had wealthy or privileged family backgrounds.[34] All others came from poor offspring, most frequently small farmers. Whether wealthy or poor, many of them capitalized on the survival skills they acquired during the Japanese occupation and added boldness, aggressiveness, speed, and flexibility. Mostly unnoticed by the outside world, a new management style was emerging in Korea: Tiger Management.

4 Globalizing Tigers

Korean companies entering the world markets

We have concluded that we will accept the challenge of a major adventure called the Middle East.

Chung Ju-yung[1]

The conditions here are impossible, but we are surviving. I know we can make it here.

A Hyundai crew leader, commenting on a construction site in Iran[2]

Pre-modern Korea was a highly isolated country, politically and economically. The "hermit kingdom" had only limited trade links with the outside world, mostly with its big neighbor, China. During the period of Japanese colonization, Korea was forced to strengthen its economic links with Japan, mainly by supplying rice and raw materials for the Japanese market and being an export market and production base for Japanese manufacturers.[3] After liberation, these trade and investment links with Japan broke down, and Korea became again an almost closed economy. Korean companies did not have much international competitiveness, and the poor and underdeveloped country was not an attractive target for foreign producers. Most imports were linked to development aid.

Since the 1960s, however, this situation has changed dramatically. With explosive growth rates, Korean companies started to export their way into the world markets. At a time when their foreign competitors had barely noticed their very existence, these companies already held respectable market shares in a wide range of manufacturing industries. And not long thereafter, they also started to invest and produce in the whole world – in North America, Europe, Asia, and elsewhere. Tiger Management made its debut on the world stage.

International trade: explosive growth since the 1960s

Overall development

Figures 4.1 and 4.2 show the development of Korea's international trade in absolute terms and in relation to the country's GDP. Exports were almost negligible until the early 1960s, amounting to less than US$50 million annually and thereby equivalent to only around one or two percent of GDP. Imports were higher, but were mostly linked to US development aid and did not reflect a foreign business interest in the Korean market.

Then, however, Korea's exports took off dramatically. They increased by twenty-five times between 1960 and 1970 and then by another twenty-one times between 1970 and 1980. In the same period, the export/GDP ratio also showed a multifold increase to more than twenty-five percent. Imports grew strongly as well and were, at latest by the 1970s, primarily driven by private business and not governmental development aid. As a result, an almost closed economy has been transformed into a fairly open economy in terms of international trade within only twenty years. Since the 1980s, both exports and imports have steadily expanded further. Most recently, Korea's exports amounted to around US$400 billion annually and thereby, more than forty percent of the country's GDP.

How could the Korean companies achieve such an exceptional export growth? One important background factor was the shift in the Korean industrial policy after 1961. As discussed in Chapter 3, the government of President Park Chung-hee dropped the import substitution policy of its predecessors and replaced it with an export promotion policy. Consequently, Korean companies that were exporting their goods to foreign markets received various subsidies, such as preferential loans, from the government during the subsequent years. Around 1970, these subsidies amounted to almost thirty percent of the total value of exports.[4]

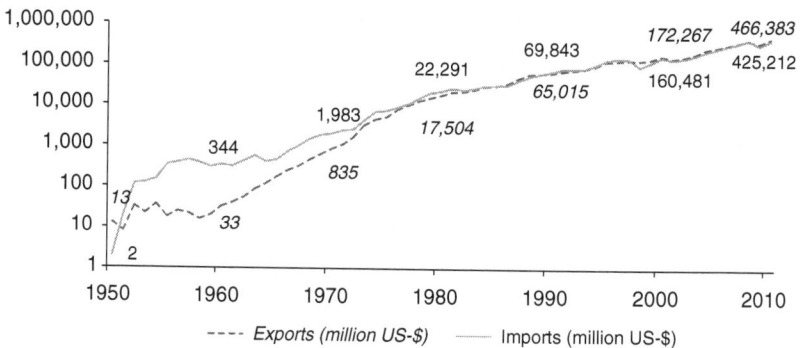

Figure 4.1 Development of Korea's exports and imports (logarithmic scale).
Source: Bank of Korea, *Economic Statistics System.*

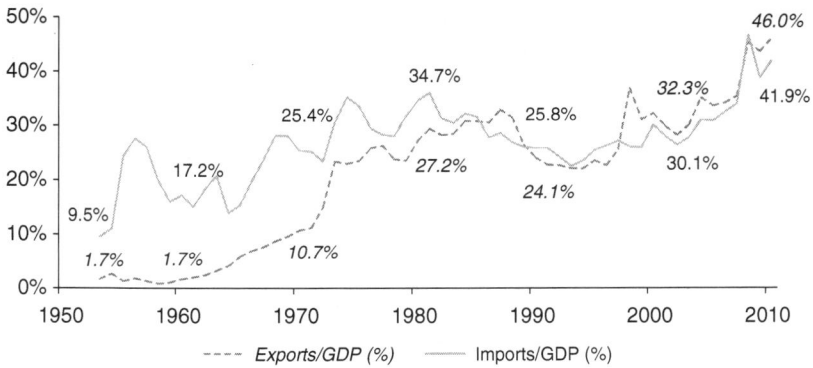

Figure 4.2 Development of Korea's exports and imports in relation to GDP.
Source: Bank of Korea, *Economic Statistics System.*

Notwithstanding this government support, however, the companies faced various obstacles that made a rapid increase in exports a very unlikely prospect.[5] Unlike their Western or Japanese competitors, they did not have a large or sophisticated home market that could serve as a test ground to sharpen competitiveness before going abroad. On account of Korea's low income level and low savings rate, the cost of capital was also higher than in most other countries. Most fundamentally, the Korean companies appeared to lack the knowledge and resources needed for launching an export business. Most of their managers did not have any international business experience or a good knowledge of English. The companies relied on collaboration with foreign competitors to acquire new technologies. Korean products were generally regarded as clearly inferior to those produced by Western and Japanese companies. In the early 1960s, international observers were extremely pessimistic regarding Korea's economic development potential.[6]

Nonetheless, many Korean companies rapidly started exporting their goods to foreign countries and succeeded against all odds. How could they achieve this? The short response is, by applying Tiger Management; which had its first debut on the domestic stage in Korea (as described in the previous chapter), also to their export business. They combined relentless efforts with a sharp-minded focus to play on whatever strengths they had and an aggressive mindset to go all out, try different approaches, and then learn by experience.

Considering that Western and Japanese competitors had a great lead in technological competencies and international business experience, what advantages had Korean companies on the world markets, after all? One such virtue was their low cost level, mostly as a result of Korea's low labor cost. Another one was the relatively high skill and education level of their workforces. Their workers were also willing and determined to do whatever was needed to achieve their companies' goals.

subsidiary was set up in New York. This step was very unusual as, at that time, US apparel companies were predominantly importing from Japan. Korean products were not regarded as competitive. Through local market research, however, Daewoo eventually understood what was needed to customize its textile products to make them more attractive for US buyers. Shortly thereafter, Daewoo started to receive orders from the US.[14]

Then, in 1972, the US government announced that it would introduce quotas for textile imports from Asia to protect its domestic industry. The quotas for each producer would be fixed in proportion to their recent import volumes. As the market shares of Korean importers were still low, the introduction of quotas was widely perceived as an effective closure of the US market. However, Daewoo took this crisis as another opportunity. The company invested heavily to ramp up its production and its exports to the US prior to the quota introduction. Such a rapid expansion was not possible on a profitable basis, as many raw materials first needed to be imported to Korea at a high price. Even though this approach appeared to be highly questionable and risky from a general viewpoint, it nicely paid off: Daewoo received a large import quota to the US that suddenly made it the largest Korean textile exporter and also allowed it to return to profitability shortly thereafter.[15]

The Samsung case

In contrast to Hyundai and Daewoo, Samsung was a "born global" business in the sense that it started as a trading company. In the years until 1960, Samsung mostly focused on obtaining import quotas for restricted goods and processing and selling them in Korea, as the market protection enabled it to make high profits with this business model. After the government introduced an export promotion policy, however, Samsung also began to make aggressive exporting efforts. Throughout the 1960s, the group's trading company exported various goods, such as sugar, canned food, apparel, yarn, and tires and thereby became the country's largest exporter.[16]

Samsung's exports became even larger and more diversified when the group branched out into electronics and shipbuilding in the 1970s. Among Korean business leaders, Samsung's Chairman, Lee Byung-chull, always placed high value on accumulating technological knowledge and therefore insisted that his researchers and engineers first needed to fully understand and master important technologies in order to create new business opportunities. Samsung's business strategies, however, were often no less aggressive than those of other *chaebols* such as Hyundai or Daewoo.

A good example is the entry of Samsung Electronics into the microwave oven business in the 1970s.[17] The product first drew the attention of a senior Samsung manager in 1976 as a potential business opportunity. It seemed unlikely that the company could ever build a successful business on this product. At the time, building microwave ovens was regarded as technologically highly demanding, and Samsung did not have the knowledge to produce them. There was no domestic market, as Koreans could not afford to buy such an expensive item. At the same time, the global microwave oven market was already well established and firmly in the hands of American and Japanese companies.

Undeterred by these facts, starting with the reverse engineering of an American-made microwave, Samsung's engineers began to develop their own product. They ran into numerous technical problems, but succeeded in producing small volumes of functioning products after just one year.

Next, when J. C. Penney looked for an OEM (original equipment manufacturer) partner to produce a low cost microwave in order to undercut the price of its competitors, Samsung seized the opportunity and entered a partnership with the Americans. It made sure that under any circumstances, delivery deadlines would always be met. While losing money on this project, Samsung thereby succeeded in entering the global microwave market.

Finally, Samsung managed to enter a joint venture with General Electric, which was losing market share to Japanese competitors. Whereas Samsung had to raise its quality standards to satisfy the American partners, it again always delivered on time. The joint venture quickly gained momentum and within a few years, its annual production has reached one million units.

Subsequently, this powerful combination of determination to engineering, low cost, and high speed paved the way to many other successes in the electronics and microelectronics industry. Samsung's most spectacular achievement was taking over the leadership in the global market for memory chips in the early 1990s.[18] Entering this very competitive industry segment as a latecomer only in the 1980s, it took global leadership in less than one decade thereafter. It succeeded because of its aggressive R&D spending and capital investment when Japanese competitors were cutting back during a global market downturn in 1990 and 1991. Moreover, Samsung also ramped up its production of each generation of new memory chips much faster than its competitors. Its competitiveness was further enhanced by various cost cutting process innovations.[19]

International investment: take-off since the 1980s

Overall development

Figure 4.3 shows the development of Korea's outward and inward direct investment. In 1980, Korean companies invested only US$45 million abroad, and the amount invested by foreign companies in Korea was only US$143 million. In other

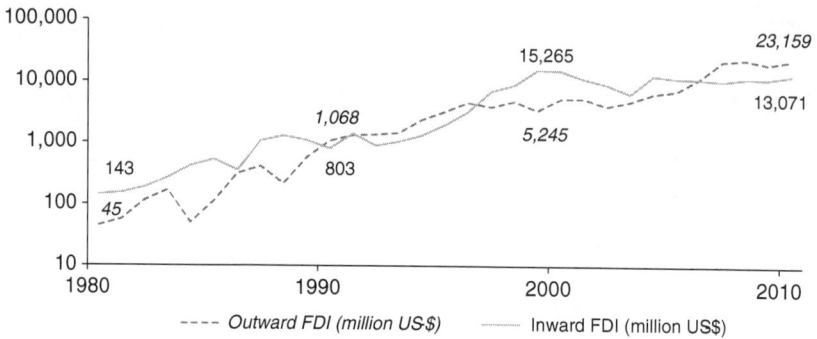

Figure 4.3 Development of Korea's outward and inward foreign direct investment (logarithmic scale).

Source: Bank of Korea, *Economic Statistics System.*

words, at a time when Korea was already fairly globalized in terms of international trade, it was still an almost closed economy in terms of international investment.

Since the 1980s, however, business investment also rapidly started to flow in and out of Korea. Inward foreign direct investment (FDI) first surpassed the mark of US$1 billion in 1988, and the same happened with outward FDI in 1990. Since then, outward FDI has continued to rise steeply and surpassed US$20 billion in every single year since 2007. Inward FDI reached a record high in the years after the 1997 Asian financial crisis and has, after falling back somewhat, stabilized in recent years at a fairly high level of more than US$10 billion annually. Altogether, a similar trend can be seen regarding Korea's international investment as for its international trade, with a time lag of around twenty years. Where international trade started its explosive growth in the 1960s, so did international investment in the 1980s. As a result, Korean companies have become major direct investors in foreign countries, while Korea itself has also become an important investment location for non-Korean companies.

What induced Korean companies to start investing abroad, in many cases, quite shortly after they had established their export business? Some initial investment, such as opening foreign sales offices or establishing dealer networks in overseas markets, was simply necessary to support their export operations. Such investment, however, was still relatively limited in its amount. The larger scale international investment that started in the 1980s, in contrast, was mostly focused on creating international production networks.

There were several reasons why Korean companies started producing abroad. First, they needed to overcome import barriers, which increasingly became obstacles for Korean exports to North America and Europe. Second, they noticed that local production generally has many advantages over exports to strengthen competitiveness in foreign markets, for example by establishing more reliable local supply chains and by customizing local production according to customer preferences. Third, offshoring production to low cost locations became increasingly important to maintain cost leadership, as the production cost in Korea was rapidly increasing with rising living standards. More fundamentally, it can be said that Korean companies started investing abroad when they noticed that there were huge opportunities in global markets. Having established export business with huge success, and having gained a certain experience in international business, they were looking for the next step to scale up their operations and become truly global players.

Notwithstanding their success in exporting, however, the question is: what enabled Korean companies to make another huge leap forward rather shortly after having started internationalizing by exporting? It needs to be kept in mind that Korea in the 1980s still had the status of a developing country. Korean companies appeared to be no match for the experienced multinationals from North America, Europe, and Japan, both technologically and financially. Moreover, in contrast to its export promotion policy, the Korean government did not provide businesses with specific support policies for overseas investment.

The answer lies, again, in the virtues of Tiger Management, which became an excellent servant to Korean firms and was also advanced and refined in the globalization process. The companies seized any opportunity that was given to them and combined boldness and determination with flexibility and speed.

Company examples

Some Korean companies already made earlier experiences with operating abroad by engaging in overseas construction projects. Hyundai Construction, which started to bid for global construction work in the late 1960s, was pioneering in this field. The company built on its experience with reconstructing war-torn infrastructure in Korea and acquired projects in locations with extremely hostile conditions such as Northern Alaska,[20] Vietnam (where construction sites were at times directly exposed to war hostilities),[21] and, later on, various Middle East countries, such as Saudi Arabia,[22] which were shunned by competitors from other countries. The company incurred heavy losses during some early projects because of its technical and managerial inexperience. For example, they built roads in Thailand during the rainy season, which were swiftly washed away thereafter, or triggered strikes by local workers who learned that their wages were very much lower than those of their Korean counterparts.[23] These early failures, however, provided invaluable experience in subsequent projects and greatly strengthened the company's competencies in the long term.

From the 1970s, some other Korean companies also began to enter the global construction business, with Daewoo being particularly aggressive in acquiring bids from developing countries with which South Korea often did not have diplomatic relations.[24] One of its first projects was conducted in Sudan, which had friendly relations with communist countries including North Korea, but no ties with South Korea. Therefore, it seemed impossible to conduct any business activity there for South Korean firms. However, after Daewoo's Chairman, Kim Woochoong, flew to Khartoum and met the Sudanese President in person, Daewoo started to receive orders. Later on, Daewoo also secured construction business worth several billion US dollars in Libya, another politically hostile country from a South Korean perspective.

Subsequently, when Korean companies started to invest directly abroad on a permanent basis, Hyundai took the lead again with its automobile business. It started building an automobile manufacturing site in the Canadian province of Quebec in 1985 to create a regional manufacturing base for the North American market.[25] This was a bold decision considering that Hyundai had just begun to export its cars to the US on a significant scale. First, the timing of the investment seemed to be perfect, as the company's North American automobile sales skyrocketed even before the local production was ramped up. By the time the plant in Canada started producing, however, sales were declining because of quality problems, which resulted in a bad reputation for the company among North American customers. Eventually, the Canadian production site had to be shut down in 1994 because of a lack of demand.[26]

Therefore, Hyundai's first attempt to localize production overseas failed – not on account of management problems at the production site, but rather as a result of the overly aggressive market entry with products that still did not have sufficient quality to succeed in North America. However, as with earlier failures, this experience greatly helped the company to succeed with subsequent investments, as it set up new production sites in Turkey, China, India, and Malaysia.[27]

Samsung was another Korean pioneer in setting up production sites overseas. It built a TV assembly plant in Portugal in 1985 in anticipation of the country's entry into the EU. Shortly thereafter, assembly plants for electronic products were also established in New Jersey and in the United Kingdom.[28] In the 1990s, additional production sites were built in China, Eastern Europe, and former Soviet Union countries.[29]

Since around 1990, other large *chaebols* have followed Hyundai's and Samsung's examples and rapidly started to internationalize their production. LG built plastic production sites in Malaysia, Indonesia, Hungary, and China, followed by a joint venture in Pakistan in 1995.[30] Daewoo started producing automobiles in Rumania, India, Poland, and China.[31]

Overall, whereas not all Korean companies and business groups began investing abroad at the same time, some common patterns can be clearly identified. First, when considering the overall modest degree of the companies' globalization, FDI started early and then was scaled up aggressively throughout the world's regions, resulting in the rapid establishment of global production networks. Second, the Korean companies eagerly learned from their early experiences and failures and swiftly changed their approaches accordingly. Whereas their first international production sites were located in advanced Western countries, they mostly focused on adding new locations in emerging and developing countries later on when they discovered that these locations might serve their needs even better. Third, they mostly established wholly owned subsidiaries when building their global networks, with joint ventures being the exception. Moreover, the majority of the production sites were newly built, rather than being acquired through the takeover of existing companies. Fourth, the senior management of overseas sites was heavily staffed with Korean expatriates.

These strategic preferences clearly express the desire of the Korean firms to control their overseas operations firmly. After all, whether inside or outside Korea, they intended to continue practicing Tiger Management, characterized by ambitious goal setting, bold decision making, immediate implementation of strategic directions, eagerness to learn, and high flexibility.

Conclusion: taking Tiger Management to the world

The analysis in this chapter has shown that Korean companies, shortly following the creation of sizeable organizations and business portfolios in their home country, rapidly began to engage in international business. From the 1960s, Korean exports grew explosively as companies started to penetrate world markets in a wide range of manufacturing industries including textiles, electronics, automobiles, and ships. Korean firms also aggressively began to acquire overseas construction projects from the late 1960s. Given their lack of resources, and of international business experience, nobody expected them to succeed except the companies themselves. However, after some early failures, they quickly gained a foothold on global markets through a combination of aggressive investment, relentless learning, outstanding speed, and high flexibility.

Thereafter, the companies took business globalization to the next level and rapidly scaled up their direct investment in foreign countries. Whereas some of this investment, such as in distribution networks, was conducted to support their export business, they also started to create international production networks very quickly to strengthen their global business presence. Again, these strategies were extremely bold when considering the companies' lack of experience with operating global business networks. However, again, they became proficient and successful in international business within a short period of time by applying a "learning by doing" approach. Undeterred by early problems and failures, they capitalized on these experiences by swiftly adjusting their practices thereafter.

Taken together, after having developed Tiger Management within Korea first, the companies rapidly internationalized and also applied their managerial approaches to their global operations. Notwithstanding some initial problems, they greatly succeeded overall. In other words, they demonstrated the effectiveness of Tiger Management to a world that only gradually took notice.

5 Struggling Tigers
The Asian financial crisis

> I think it was the financial crisis that literally put Samsung at the edge of dying, that forced them to rethink everything. Yes, initially there was a major resistance, a major barrier, but on the other hand because of the Asian financial crisis there was also the view that they had no other choice. There was nothing else they could do but this.
>
> Eric Kim, former Chief Marketing Officer, Samsung Electronics[1]

In the 1990s, after three decades of explosive growth, the future of Korean companies looked brighter than ever. They had transformed themselves from local players in a poor developing country to strong global competitors commanding not only vast human, financial, and technological assets, but also occupying high global market shares in a wide range of advanced manufacturing industries such as steel, shipbuilding, automobiles, electronics, and microelectronics. Competitors in Western countries and in Japan eventually woke up to the challenge the Korean companies posed to them and realized they had to take them very seriously. For the first time, the outside world developed an interest in how Korean companies were organized and managed, as documented by various books on this subject published in English during the 1990s.[2] In short, Korean companies were the rising stars in the global business world.

Then, however, the Asian financial crisis suddenly struck Korea in 1997. It started in South-East Asia, a quite distant region from a Korean viewpoint – first with a financial crisis in Thailand, followed by similar problems in Malaysia and Indonesia. At that time, few people anticipated that the crisis would have a severe impact on Korea, as the Korean economy was much more advanced and developed than those of the South-East Asian countries first affected by it. However, when the crisis arrived in Korea, it turned out to be devastating for many Korean companies as well as for the Korean economy as a whole. As will be discussed in this chapter, these companies did not merely have "bad luck," but were also paying the price for their failure to adjust to a changing business environment. At the same time, however, the crisis induced the Korean companies to take drastic steps to restructure and strengthen their organization and management. As a result, the majority of companies that survived the crisis created, in effect, a more advanced and sophisticated version of Tiger Management when compared with the pre-crisis situation.

The unfolding of the crisis

The Asian financial crisis started rather unpretentiously as a local currency crisis in Thailand in July 1997, when the Thai government was forced to abandon the peg of the Baht with the US dollar, resulting in a sudden collapse of the Baht's exchange rate. In the preceding months, the Baht came repeatedly under speculative pressure, as it was generally regarded as overvalued. Thailand had been piling up huge amounts of foreign debt and ran a large current account deficit for several years. After the plunge of the exchange rate, the Thai economy collapsed, as many debtors failed to serve payments on their foreign debt, which were much higher now when valued in local currency.[3] Soon after the currency crisis in Thailand, the currencies of Malaysia and Indonesia also came under strong pressure, eventually resulting in drastic devaluations. In both countries, large scale sell-offs on the stock markets and severe economic recessions followed.

From a Korean perspective, one might expect that the crisis in South-East Asia would have been regarded as an event with rather limited impact for the domestic economy, as the affected countries were not Korea's most important trading partners and all were developing countries; whereas Korea had a much more advanced economy and had already joined the OECD (Organization for Economic Co-operation and Development) in 1996. Notwithstanding the country's more advanced economic status, however, investors in Korea were already nervous in 1997, as one business group (Hanbo) went bankrupt and another one (Kia) asked the government for emergency loans.[4] After the financial crisis broke out in South-East Asia during the summer, a spillover to Korea looked more and more likely as the Korean Won was also regarded as overvalued and the country ran a current account deficit. As a consequence, capital outflows accelerated during summer and fall of 1997.

Eventually, the Bank of Korea almost depleted its foreign exchange reserves and could not defend the external value of its currency any further, causing the exchange rate of the Won against major currencies to halve within a few days. This sudden and extreme currency devaluation steeply increased the burden of Korean debtors in foreign currencies. Moreover, foreign creditors became reluctant to roll over expiring loans to Korean companies and forced them to repay their debt.

The liquidity crisis thereby accelerated and eventually forced the government to seek the IMF's (International Monetary Fund) financial assistance on 21 November 1997 to avoid a default of the country on its foreign debt.[5] The IMF subsequently stepped in, but also required the Korean government to launch an austerity program and implement various structural reforms to restore macroeconomic stability. As a result, companies were subsequently forced to reduce their debt with domestic financial institutions.

The financial crisis delivered a triple financial punch to Korean companies: (1) an increasing burden to service their foreign debt because of the devaluation of the Korean Won; (2) the need to repay foreign debt, as foreign creditors became reluctant to extend their loans; and (3) the need to reduce their domestic debt as a consequence of the Korean government reforms imposed by the IMF. Overall, these financial constraints proved to be too much for many among them. As can be seen from Table 5.1, no less than nine out of the country's thirty largest business groups either went bankrupt or were forced into bank-financed restructuring programs until 2000, excluding Hanbo which already defaulted before the crisis became imminent. Among the victims was Daewoo Group, which was the country's fourth largest *chaebol* at that time. The bankruptcies and restructuring programs resulted in large scale layoffs which further aggravated the crisis. Consequently, the country's real GDP shrank by 5.7 percent in 1998.[6]

Underlying reasons for the failures of Korean companies

The review of the 1997 Asian financial crisis and its impact on Korea in the previous section shows that Korean companies were primarily affected by various developments on the international financial markets that were out of their control. Were their financial difficulties and bankruptcies, then, solely the result of a massive amount of bad luck?

The answer to this question is clearly "no." Whereas the financial crisis certainly exposed Korean companies to a quite extreme "stress test," the severe outcomes also showed that many of these companies were extremely vulnerable to such external shocks. In fact, the crisis laid open various structural weaknesses of Korean firms which were mostly linked to major shifts in the competitive environment they operated in and to which many of them did not sufficiently adapt.

One underlying factor which undermined the competitiveness of Korean companies was the steeply rising labor cost in Korea which reflected the country's economic success and its rising living standards. Therefore, to maintain their cost competitiveness, many companies speeded up the globalization of their operations, including the setup of manufacturing facilities in low cost countries and regions such as China or South-East Asia.[7] Such a rapid expansion created strong

Table 5.1 Number of member firms of Korea's thirty largest business groups in 1997 and 2000

Rank in 1997	Name	Number of member firms	
		Year 1997	Year 2000
1	Hyundai	57	35
2	Samsung	80	45
3	LG	49	43
4	Daewoo	30	Bankrupt
5	SK	46	39
6	Ssangyong	25	22
7	Hanjin	24	18
8	Kia	28	Bankrupt
9	Hanwha	31	23
10	Lotte	30	28
11	Kumho	26	20
12	Halla	18	Bankrupt
13	Dongah	19	16
14	Doosan	25	16
15	Daelim	21	18
16	Hansol	23	19
17	Hyosung	18	13
18	Dongkuk Steel	17	14
19	Jinro	24	16
20	Kolon	24	17
21	Kohap	13	6
22	Dongbu	34	19
23	Tongyang	24	25
24	Haetai	15	Bankrupt
25	Newcore	18	Workout
26	Anam	21	14
27	Hanil	7	Bankrupt
28	Geopyung	22	Bankrupt
29	Daesang	25	Reorganization
30	Sinho	25	Workout

Source: Korea Fair Trade Commission, *Companies affiliated with large business groups*.

Note: "Workout" indicates a restructuring program under government supervision, whereas "reorganization" indicates self-organized restructuring.

financing needs, and these needs were mostly met through debt financing rather than equity financing. As a result, the average debt-equity ratio of the country's thirty largest business groups exceeded 600 percent in 1997, with some of them having debt-equity ratios of almost 4,000 percent.[8] Moreover, a significant part of this debt was borrowed not in Korea, but in foreign countries, thereby creating an exchange rate risk in addition to the general risk of debt financing. These financial vulnerabilities proved to be fatal for many *chaebols* during the crisis.

The over-indebtedness of many Korean business groups was exacerbated by a system of group-internal mutual debt guarantees through which the repayment of the debt of specific group companies was guaranteed by other group companies. These mutual guarantees were practiced so extensively in some *chaebols* that nobody could really guarantee the debt any longer when the financial crisis set in. As a result, there were domino effects once some group companies that also guaranteed the debt of other group companies went bankrupt. One extreme case of such bankruptcy spillovers was Daewoo Group. When the group collapsed in 1999, all its member companies defaulted at the same time because of mutual debt guarantees.[9]

Moreover, there were various other weaknesses that further aggravated the companies' problems. One such weakness was over-diversification, particularly in unrelated business areas that had few synergies with a group's other activities. A well-known case of such failed diversification was Samsung's venture into the automobile sector, an industry which was already plagued by global over-capacity during the 1990s. The diversification decision was made in 1994, and after an automobile factory was built, production started in 1998 – in the midst of the economic crisis. The group's automobile company continued to make losses, went bankrupt in 1999, and was sold to Renault in 2000. Whereas the unfortunate timing of the business' launch was certainly the result of factors beyond management's control, it is also widely believed that the diversification was fundamentally unsound, as Samsung had no experience whatsoever in the automobile business, and the synergies with its other businesses were very limited.[10]

Another problem that plagued some Korean companies was their burgeoning internal bureaucracy, which decreased their organizational dynamism and stifled the creativity of their employees.[11] On account of lengthy and bureaucratic internal planning and approval procedures, the improvisation skills, which were previously a major competitive weapon of Korean companies in uncertain and dynamic business environments, could be played out less and less effectively.

Finally, some Korean companies also faced serious leadership problems. Arguably, one major factor that contributed to Daewoo's downfall in 1999 was the insufficient communication between Chairman Kim Woo-choong and his subordinates during the final years before bankruptcy.[12] Chairman Kim certainly sensed the need for major organizational changes as Daewoo Group had grown quickly and became a highly globalized business. Therefore, he gave directions to reorganize the group into regional units in an effort to reduce complexity and increase local responsiveness in each country and region. However, managers received little concrete information and explanation on how this reorganization should be implemented. As a result, confusion and rumors spread throughout the whole group, generating chaos and making the restructuring counter-productive. This aggravated the crisis which resulted in the bankruptcy and dismantling of the whole group.

Daewoo's case, though extreme regarding the scale of the ultimate disaster, was not necessarily an untypical one in terms of leadership crisis. As discussed in the preceding chapters, Korean companies rapidly expanded under the personal leadership of their chairmen, which often was very effective when the companies were still relatively small and subordinate managers were the long-term associates of the chairmen and could understand their directions well, however "cryptic" they were. In the much larger and more globalized organizations the groups had been transformed into by the 1990s, however, giving such vague guidance became less and less effective or even harmful.

Some *chaebols* were also plagued by different leadership problems when the first generation chairmen retired and executive responsibility was passed on to the next generation, mostly the sons of the companies' founders. Not all of these successors had the same charisma, passion, and capabilities as their fathers, arguably resulting in a deterioration of leadership quality in some Korean business groups.

Taken together, notwithstanding the external origins of the Asian financial crisis, its severe impact laid bare the vulnerability of Korean companies to such external shocks. In the 1990s, many *chaebols* committed two managerial sins that made them extremely vulnerable: an overstretching of their resources, and a lack of adaption to a rapidly changing environment.

The crisis management of Korean companies

Restructuring

The financial crisis triggered a major restructuring of Korean business groups. Some of these efforts were led by the government following the restructuring guidelines imposed by the IMF as a condition for its financial assistance.[13] Practically, much of this restructuring was implemented through banks, which were effectively nationalized during the crisis.

One specific objective was to reduce the groups' debt-equity ratios to restore their financial credibility. Steady progress was made regarding this goal: the average debt-equity ratio of the largest five *chaebols* was reduced to 212.0 percent until the end of 1999 and, later on, to 131.4 percent in 2004. For the thirty largest *chaebols*, the debt-ratios went down to 393.7 percent in 1999 and to 210.6 percent in 2004.[14] Aside from repaying debt, many groups reduced their debt-equity ratios by an equity increase through the revaluation of real estate and security holdings.

Another policy to restore the groups' credibility was the termination of group-internal mutual debt guarantees that undermined the *chaebols'* financial soundness, as discussed earlier in this chapter. This goal was also quite rapidly achieved, as the four largest *chaebols* abandoned all such guarantees until the end of 2000.[15]

Furthermore, the government initiated corporate workout programs in order to liquidate quickly the non-viable companies while restoring the health of financially troubled yet fundamentally competitive businesses. Until 1999, fifty-four companies entered such workouts, out of which twenty-nine were liquidated until November 2000.[16]

Finally, the government also initiated a "Big Deal" plan to induce business groups to merge or swap certain companies and operations in order to create more focused groups, tightly organized around their core activities. One major case of such cross-group restructuring was the handover of LG Semiconductor to Hyundai Electronics to create a more competitive semiconductor company (later named Hynix Semiconductor), another case was the joint establishment of a new business entity in the railroad vehicle industry by Hyundai, Daewoo, and Hanjin (later named Hyundai Rotem). Many envisioned business deals, however, could not be realized, while others were not successful in terms of the new companies' business performance. For example, Hynix Semiconductor could only survive after the government pressured financial institutions to buy its bonds. One underlying problem with the Big Deal plan appears to have been its rapid implementation without sufficient study of the real synergy effects that could potentially be achieved.[17]

Aside from a few widely discussed cases under the Big Deal plan, however, most *chaebols* restructured their group companies during the crisis quite aggressively anyway. As shown in Table 5.1, all of the thirty largest groups in 1997 reduced their number of affiliated companies in the following three years, with only one exception (Tongyang Group). Overall, the number of affiliated companies of the thirty largest business groups decreased from 819 in 1997 to 544 in 2000.[18] Also, most business groups became more focused during this period. The percentage of total sales falling to each group's core activities increased considerably.[19]

Some cases of group level reorganization were not directly induced by the crisis. However, even in these cases, the crisis situation and the perceived need to create more focused business groups resulted in outcomes which may not have occurred otherwise. The most prominent case was the break-up of Hyundai Group in the year 2000 among the heirs of its founder, Chung Ju-yung, into two smaller groups. One of these groups, named Hyundai Motor Group, was focused on the automobile and steel business, whereas the other part, which kept the name Hyundai Group, carried over the remaining business interests.[20]

Another major *chaebol* restructuring occurred a few years later, when LG Group spun off its copper smelting, electric wire, and electric power equipment businesses into a newly created LS Group in 2003. Furthermore, a variety of other businesses centered on oil refining, construction, and distribution were separated into the new and independent GS Group in 2005. The remaining LG Group thereafter mainly focused its business on activities related to electronics and chemicals.[21]

Taken together, it can be seen that, whereas some important restructuring of Korean business groups was first initiated by the government during the crisis, most groups made major indigenous efforts to reorganize their portfolio of business activities in the years after 1997 to divest peripheral interests and re-focus on a limited number of core industries. Moreover, a comparison of those groups that survived the crisis with those that went bankrupt reveals that *chaebols* belonging to the former group were clearly more aggressive in streamlining their business portfolios than those in the latter group. This indicates that the shakeout during the crisis worked as a selection mechanism among the *chaebols* in which only those groups survived that were capable of streamlining their business portfolios and disposing of assets unrelated to their core activities.[22]

The business groups also disposed some of their international joint ventures during the crisis, possibly to concentrate on those operations over which they had full managerial control. At the same time, however, they set up new collaborations with foreign companies when they saw new business opportunities. For example, LG Group sold its fifty percent stake in LG Honeywell to its American partner in 1999, but created a new venture with Japan's Nikko in the copper business in the same year.[23] This eagerness to explore new business opportunities with foreign partners is remarkable when keeping in mind that *chaebols* were under severe financial distress in the years after 1997.

Overall, there was a clear tendency among most business groups to concentrate the restructuring on peripheral or non-viable domestic operations and to preserve international business interests to the maximum possible extent. One underlying reason for the *chaebols'* primarily domestic retrenchment was the intensifying competition in Korea as the government opened the country's market to non-Korean companies as a part of its bailout agreement with the IMF. However, Korean executives also perceived an increased globalization of their business activities as a possible way to overcome the crisis.[24]

Managerial reforms

Aside from restructuring efforts, Korean firms and business groups also introduced various managerial reforms during the economic crisis. In one major area, the government played a leading role: corporate governance. As the lack of transparency regarding the *chaebols'* ownership and management structures was seen as a major reason for the crisis, the government felt a strong need to improve the business groups' corporate governance.

In the years after 1997, various new laws were enacted to achieve this goal.[25] All stock-market listed firms were required to appoint at least two outside directors, and large firms with total assets exceeding two trillion Won at least three. New accounting rules in line with international standards were introduced and business groups that exceeded the asset threshold value of two trillion Won also needed to report consolidated financial statements where group-internal transactions were canceled out. Furthermore, corporate laws were changed to strengthen the rights of minority shareholders. Finally, *chaebol* chairmen, who effectively exerted a strong managerial influence on group companies, were now regarded as de facto directors of these companies even without holding formal managerial positions and thereby made legally accountable for the outcomes of the companies' business strategies.

Overall, the legal changes introduced by the government certainly had a significant impact on the *chaebols'* corporate governance and increased their transparency both in quantitative and in qualitative terms, though there is still an ongoing debate regarding the extent to which the groups' governance structures really have improved.[26] This issue will be further discussed in Chapter 11.

Separate from the need to follow legal amendments introduced by the government, however, Korean companies also conducted major efforts to adjust their management systems to the changing business environment in which they were operating. They streamlined their organizations to become more efficient and dynamic again. As discussed in the previous section, they consolidated many subsidiaries on the group level. This helped them to simplify organizational structures and reduce the doubling of efforts. Such organizational consolidation was also conducted within individual companies to decrease the number of departments and organizational units.[27]

Moreover, the companies also changed the way they dealt with their managers and workers. Under the pressure of the crisis, the previously common de facto employment guarantee given to regular employees by large companies could no longer be maintained. Many companies conducted massive layoffs to cut cost and secure their survival. For example, Samsung Electronics reduced its workforce by one third from 60,000 to 40,000 in the years after 1997.[28]

Many companies also changed incentive structures for their managers and workers to boost their efficiency. As will be discussed in more detail in Chapter 9, the previously common seniority-based compensation and promotion systems were rapidly transformed to reward systems which strongly reflected individual performance. Whereas some groups, such as Samsung, had already started creating such new systems since earlier in the 1990s, their implementation was accelerated during the years of the crisis.[29]

The second Tiger generation: the emergence of venture companies

An additional factor which contributed to the transformation of Korean industry during the crisis and created the base for future growth was the emergence of a new generation of innovative companies. During previous decades, the Korean economy was strongly dominated by *chaebols*. Small- and medium-sized enterprises (SMEs) were clearly subordinated to these business groups by either working as their suppliers or focusing on local industries not deemed attractive by the *chaebols*, such as small-scale retailing or restaurants. As a consequence of the Korean education boom, which produced a high number of skilled university graduates and financial deregulation, however, an increasing number of innovative venture firms emerged from the 1990s. These firms created their own business models independently from the *chaebols*, often focusing on technology intensive products and services.

The financial crisis proved to be a huge opportunity for these companies for two reasons. First, as the dominance of the Korean economy by *chaebols* was widely perceived as a major reason for the crisis, the government eagerly provided venture firms with generous financial support programs to diminish this *chaebol* dominance in the years after 1997. Second, as a consequence of the crisis, the venture firms also suddenly had access to highly skilled human resources not available previously when the graduates of elite universities all lined up to find jobs in prestigious companies. Now, such career opportunities in the business groups were becoming very scarce, as the *chaebols* hired few new employees, and at the same time looked increasingly unattractive given the groups' financial difficulties and tainted public image. Moreover, many *chaebols* also had to lay off managers and engineers, adding to the pool of highly skilled job seekers venture firms could tap into.

The creation of some major venture firms was the direct outcome of the economic crisis. Seven former Samsung managers founded ReignCom (which later changed its name to iriver) in 1999 to create their own business. Within just a few years, they developed it into a sizable producer of portable music players.[30] Another group of engineers who left Samsung during the crisis created Naver, now Korea's leading Internet portal.[31]

Other venture firms were founded earlier, and thrived during the financial crisis. One well-known example is AhnLab, a producer of Internet security software founded in 1995 by Ahn Cheol-soo, who was a pioneer in creating virus protection programs for computers. The company quickly became the dominant player in its field in Korea and also expanded into many other countries.[32]

Notably, these and other venture companies also relied on the virtues of Tiger Management by boldly proposing new ideas and aggressively seizing business opportunities. What distinguished them from the first generation *chaebols* was the very strong educational background and professionalism of their founders and executives and their approach in developing their businesses, which was more focused in terms of product lines and more global from the outset in terms of geographic coverage. As such, a second generation of Tigers emerged which helped not only to transform the Korean economy, but also to advance and modernize Tiger Management. Further examples of such companies and their globalization are given in Chapter 6.

Conclusion: how the Asian financial crisis advanced Tiger Management

This chapter has looked at the impact the Asian financial crisis had on Korean companies. It put all of them under extreme financial distress and forced many business groups into bankruptcy or reorganization.

Whereas the financial crisis first broke out in South-East Asia, were there also various internal reasons that explained why its impact was so serious in Korea. Many *chaebols*, under pressure to retain international competitiveness as their domestic labor cost was increasing, had invested aggressively abroad and therefore mostly relied on debt financing, which they were accustomed to from their early days. However, in contrast to the 1960s and 1970s, a significant part of their debt was now held by foreign creditors. Moreover, even in Korea itself, the financial sector was gradually liberalized, and the government became reluctant to guarantee the companies' debt and bail them out if necessary. In other words, debt financing became much riskier over time, but many Korean firms did not sufficiently consider this increased risk.

Additionally, the organization and management of many *chaebols* also did not reflect their bigger size and more globalized business environment. In the 1960s and 1970s, the business groups could still primarily rely on the domestic Korean market, which offered excellent business opportunities on account of its high growth and widespread shielding from international competition by the government. Moreover, many groups' portfolios of business interests were still relatively limited at that time (see Tables 3.1 to 3.5). Under such conditions, the paternalistic leadership style of their chairmen proved to be extremely effective, as discussed in the preceding two chapters.

In the 1980s and 1990s, however, many *chaebols* had turned themselves into large and highly diversified global players. The groups' much larger size and globalization demanded a more formally organized and professional management style. However, many *chaebols* still heavily relied on the personal leadership of their chairmen, which turned out to be less and less effective.

In short, many Korean companies and groups kept relying on the version of Tiger Management that they had built throughout the previous decades, and failed to adapt it to a less protected, more competitive and more globalized business environment. This failure made them vulnerable to external shocks, and the Asian financial crisis proved to be a strong external shock that brutally exposed the *chaebols'* weaknesses.

When facing the crisis, however, most business groups re-discovered competitive weapons that had previously helped in making them great: speed and flexibility (the ability to adapt quickly to changing circumstances) as well as boldness (the ability to act decisively).

Most *chaebols* made rapid and far-reaching efforts to consolidate their portfolios of business interests, in particular, to sell off unrelated or non-profitable activities and merge and consolidate others. Moreover, they also readjusted their organization and management. Organizational structures were streamlined to increase the speed of decision-making and implementation of managerial policies again. The companies also abandoned employment guarantees and laid off many workers and managers. Furthermore, they rapidly introduced performance orientated promotion and compensation schemes, which replaced the previous systems that mainly focused on seniority.

In essence, Tiger Management was readjusted during the crisis to bring it in line with the very different business environment the companies were now operating in. Thereby, notwithstanding the adverse conditions under which they operated in the years after 1997, many of them not just survived the crisis, but left it with leaner business portfolios, more efficient organizational structures, and modernized management systems. It can also be said that the shakeout induced by the crisis worked as a selection mechanism among Korean business groups. Those *chaebols* that were not sufficiently capable or willing to adjust to the new environment were broken up or reorganized, whereas those that successfully adapted themselves reinforced their global competitiveness.

In sum, the Asian financial crisis laid open the hidden vulnerabilities of Korean business groups and starkly showed the need to adjust Tiger Management to a more open, competitive, global, and risky business environment. In effect, however, the crisis also resulted in an advancement of Tiger Management, as those companies that adjusted to the new competitive environment were fundamentally strengthened, whereas those that did not disappeared from the competitive landscape. In addition, a new generation of Korean companies emerged which also represented a modernized, professionalized, and globalized version of Tiger Management.

6 Revitalized Tigers

Korean companies in the twenty-first century

Let's leave Korea behind us and now be reborn as a global top level company.

Lee Kun-hee[1]

How have Korean companies performed in recent years after overcoming the shock of the Asian financial crisis? And how has Tiger Management evolved in the twenty-first century? These are the themes this chapter will focus on.

Overall, Korean companies did extremely well throughout the last decade. After consolidating their balance sheets and business portfolios, and adjusting their management systems to a more globalized and competitive environment, they started growing rapidly again. At the same time, they achieved and sustained a high profitability while avoiding a fall back into risky debt financing.

As the domestic Korean market became saturated in most industries, the companies' growth was mainly derived from international business. Korean companies rapidly localized their operations in the leading markets of the world economy, notably North America and Europe, and at the same time aggressively scaled up their activities in large emerging markets such as China and India. As a result, they moved into the global top ranks in a variety of manufacturing industries, including automobiles, microelectronics, consumer electronics, steel, and shipbuilding. They retained all original virtues of Tiger Management (aggressiveness, speed, flexibility, and perseverance) while constantly readjusting their management to the new challenges they faced over the years.

The overall performance of Korean companies in the last decade will be analyzed in this chapter, followed by a discussion of their most recent wave of globalization. Thereafter, the companies' recent developments will be illustrated with various case examples.

Korean companies' overall performance

Figure 6.1 shows overall performance indicators of Korean companies over the last decade. Korean firms have maintained a ratio of operating income to sales of above 5 percent, in every year, since the turn of the millennium. This performance compares favorably with that of firms from leading advanced countries, such as the US, Japan, and Germany.[2] Furthermore, the Korean companies reduced their ratio of interest expenses to sales from 4 percent in 2000 to less than 2 percent in 2003, indicating a much improved financial stability. At the same time, they also recorded an increase in overall sales in every year, including the global recession years of 2001 and 2009. The average annual sales growth rate over the last decade amounted to 8.5 percent, underlining the companies' strong overall performance.

Moreover, Korean companies did not only perform generally well in the first decade of the twenty-first century, but also clearly did better than their competitors from other countries. As can be seen from Figure 6.2, they greatly increased their global market shares in a wide range of advanced manufacturing industries, including growth sectors such as semiconductors and mobile phones as well as mature sectors such as automobiles and shipbuilding.

Overall, the data show that Korean companies posted very healthy financial results and, at the same time, made great advances in their global market positions. In the following section, it will be shown how this international growth was achieved.

The accelerated globalization of Korean companies

Global market penetration

Korean companies rapidly continued to increase their global market presence after the turn of the millennium. Throughout the first decade of the twenty-first century, the country's exports increased by 2.7 times from US$172.3 billion in 2000 to US$466.4 billion in 2010 (see Figure 4.1).

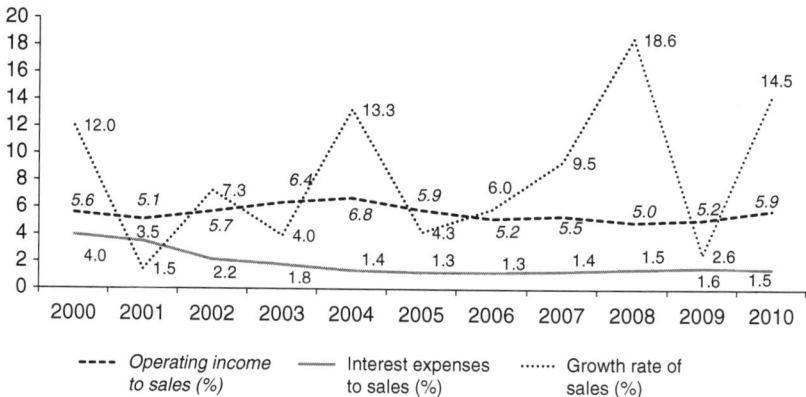

Figure 6.1 Indicators of Korean companies' financial performance, 2000–2010.
Source: Bank of Korea, *Economic Statistics System*.

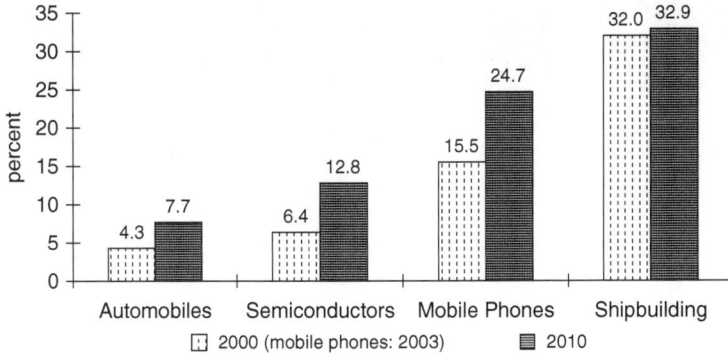

Figure 6.2 Korean companies' global market shares in selected industries.

Sources: OICA, World Ranking of Manufacturers; iSuppli, Market Watch; Gartner, Gartner Newsroom; SAJ, Shipbuilding Statistics.

Figure 6.3 shows the major destinations of Korea's exports. The Asia Pacific region, which was already Korea's largest export destination in 2000, became even more important thereafter with a threefold increase until 2010. More than half of Korean exports went to this region, with China (including Hong Kong) alone accounting for 30.5 percent of all exports. In contrast, exports to North America increased at a more modest rate, with a growth of 35 percent in value between 2000 and 2010. Exports to European countries approximately doubled during this period. Korea also more than tripled its exports to Latin America and the Middle East. Whereas the overall weight of these regions among the country's exports is still a minor one, Korea exported goods worth more than US$10 billion to each of them by 2010, indicating an increased market presence of its companies.

Overall, the companies have increased their exports to all regions of the world throughout the last decade. However, they have achieved a particularly strong export growth to the Asia Pacific, Latin America, and Middle East regions, which are mostly populated by emerging and developing economies. Whereas exports to North America and Europe increased, most of the overall growth of export volume came from the Asia Pacific region. As a result, Korean companies, which previously focused more on the North American and European markets in their international business, have now established major market positions in all regions of the world.

Localization

While increasing their global market presence, Korean companies stepped up their direct investment in foreign countries even more rapidly. Korea's FDI (foreign direct investment) jumped from US$5.25 billion in 2000 to US$23.16 billion in 2010 (see Figure 4.3) and thereby increased by no less than 340 percent within only one decade.

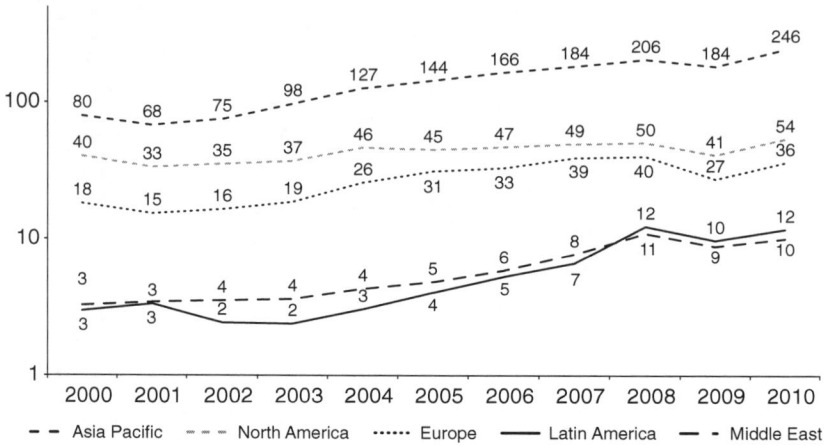

Figure 6.3 Korean companies' exports by region (in billion US$, logarithmic scale).

Source: Bank of Korea, *Economic Statistics System.*

Figure 6.4 shows the composition of FDI by regions. Similarly to Korean exports, the Asia Pacific region became the largest investment location for Korean companies since the turn of the millennium. In fact, they invested more than US$10 billion in this region alone in every single year since 2007. At the same time, however, investment into other regions also showed a multi-fold increase. Throughout the last several years, Korean companies annually invested approximately US$5 billion each in North America and Europe. Direct investment in Latin America, the Middle East, and Africa, while still lagging behind in volume compared with other regions, also grew rapidly.

Taken together, the data show that Korean companies maintained rapid growth by expanding their international business. Exports increased with annual rates of 10–20 percent, and foreign direct investment expanded even more steeply. As a result, Korean companies rapidly localized their international business by building local production and distribution networks, particularly in the Asia Pacific, North American, and European regions.

In the next section, specific examples will be given of how Korean companies revitalized themselves in recent years by expanding their international business. These case examples include both established *chaebol* companies and more recently founded venture companies.

Case examples of Tiger companies in the twenty-first century

Chaebol Tigers

Korea's three biggest *chaebols* (Samsung, Hyundai Motor, and LG) all have flagship companies that hold dominant positions within their respective business

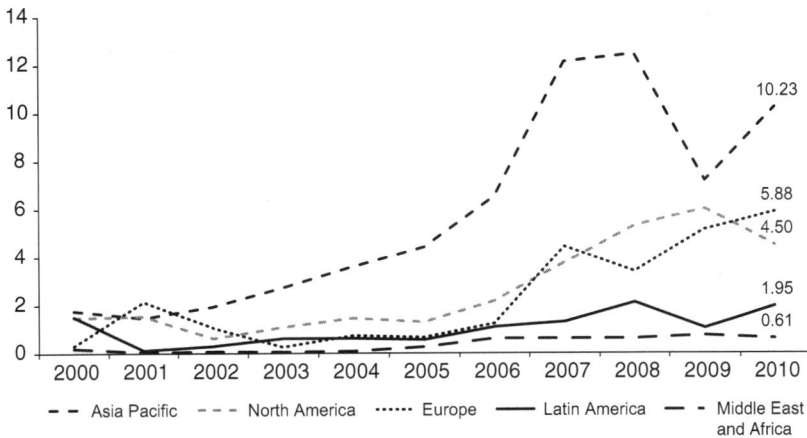

Figure 6.4 Korean companies' foreign direct investment by region (in billion US$).
Source: Bank of Korea, *Economic Statistics System.*

groups: Samsung Electronics, Hyundai Motor, and LG Electronics. All three of these companies have recorded remarkable growth and many other achievements throughout the last decade.

Samsung Electronics

As discussed in Chapter 4, Samsung Electronics had already achieved a global leadership position in one industry segment by the early 1990s: memory chips. Its various other electronic products, however, were little known outside Korea. One major reason for this obscurity was that Samsung was engaged for many years in contract manufacturing for other companies rather than selling its products under its own brand. Moreover, Samsung had not localized its production in overseas markets yet and primarily relied on exports from Korea.

In order to overcome these limitations, to save labor cost, and to create a stronger global market presence, Samsung built five large manufacturing complexes from the mid 1990s. These complexes are located in Mexico, Malaysia, the UK, China, and Brazil and all produce a wide range of Samsung's products, ranging from TV sets to monitors to mobile phones to household appliances, to serve customer demand in each major region. Moreover, additional production sites were built in countries neighboring the locations of these large complexes to allow regional synergies.[3] At the same time, key suppliers such as Samsung Electro-Mechanics, Samsung SDI, and Samsung Corning were integrated into the complexes, resulting in a high degree of vertical integration.[4]

This horizontally and vertically integrated international localization of production provided Samsung with various advantages over its global competitors who had a lower degree of integration at their overseas manufacturing sites. First, it enabled flexible resource sharing and synergies among the operations in each complex. Second, it allowed Samsung to transfer its manufacturing systems from Korea to other countries with relative ease as less local adjustment was needed for such integrated operations; compared with less integrated systems that relied to a higher extent on external partners. Third, Samsung established a stable supply chain in each region, whereas competitors relying on external suppliers often encountered serious difficulties in emerging economies such as China.[5]

At the same time, Samsung also intensified its efforts in global marketing and branding. It unified its previously scattered brands into a single global brand and poured a large amount of resources into international marketing campaigns in each major market.[6] As a result, the global awareness and perception of the Samsung brand rapidly moved up the ranks. According to Interbrand, it ranked nineteenth among all global brands in 2010 compared to forty-second in 2001.[7]

Samsung also made vast efforts to strengthen its competencies in research and development (R&D) and design. Its R&D workforce and expenses have multiplied since the 1990s. The company has also created various design centers around the world to catch global trends and ideas. These investments paid off very visibly. Samsung Electronics became a leading global patent producer, second in the world only to IBM.[8] At the same time, it began to pick up numerous design awards from leading institutions in the US, Europe, and Japan.[9]

In short, Samsung Electronics went all out from the late 1990s to invest comprehensively into global production and marketing networks as well as into its research, development, and design competencies. These deep and bold investments elevated the company from a relatively unknown hardware manufacturer to a leading player in all markets where it competes. It now holds the global number one position in LCD panels and flat panel TVs and the number two position in mobile phones, while at the same time keeping its leading position in memory chips. It posts strong profits every year, and its sales are well balanced between all major global markets, with 28.1 percent coming from America, 23.4 percent from Europe, 16.7 percent from Korea, 15.7 percent from China, and 16.1 percent from other Asian countries in 2010.[10] Samsung Electronics has apparently outperformed its global competitors. It has become not only Korea's largest company, but also the world's largest technology company.[11]

Hyundai Motor

Hyundai Motor is the core company of the Hyundai Motor *chaebol,* the largest successor of the former Hyundai group, which was broken up in 2000 as explained in Chapter 5. At the same time, it is the only remaining independent Korean automobile company, as its rivals were sold off during the Asian financial crisis, either to non-Korean carmakers or taken over by Hyundai Motor itself.

Hyundai Motor has been well known in Korea since the 1970s, when it showed exceptional dynamism in scaling up its operations domestically and internationally (see Chapter 4 for a detailed description). However, from a global viewpoint, it was still a modest second tier player as recently as the 1990s. Its production volume was only a fraction of that of leading carmakers from the US, Europe, and Japan. Its first attempt to establish an overseas production site in Canada ended in a failure in 1994.[12]

Since then, however, Hyundai Motor has managed to become one of the four largest automobile companies in the world. Its first major expansion move was the acquisition of bankrupt Kia Motor Corporation during the Asian financial crisis in 1998, which added approximately 50 percent volume to Hyundai's production capacity. After the acquisition, while keeping the Kia subsidiary and brand separate, the two companies' operations were quickly integrated.[13]

Overall, however, the primary source of the company's growth in recent years became its international expansion. Soon after the closure of its production plant in Canada, it began investing abroad again. It opened new production sites in Turkey (1997), India (1998), China (2002), the US (2005), the Czech Republic (2008), and Russia (2011). Moreover, the Kia Motor subsidiary started producing in China (2002), Slovakia (2006), and the US (2009). An additional Hyundai factory is under construction in Brazil and scheduled to open in late 2012.[14] As a result, Hyundai Motor will have local production plants in North America, Europe, and in all four BRIC (Brazil, Russia, India, and China) economies. In other words, it has localized its production in all major automobile markets of the world. The company's overseas production ratio has increased from close to zero in the 1990s to more than 50 percent in 2011.[15]

Aside from this breathtaking speed of international expansion and localization, which was all achieved through greenfield investments, it is noteworthy that Hyundai Motor has not just been growing in numbers, but also rapidly moved up the global ranks in terms of productivity and quality. As recently as the 1990s, it had a low quality reputation, particularly in North America. In recent years, however, it has entered the global top ranks of various productivity and quality ratings, such as those of the Harbour Report and J D Power.[16] As a consequence, the company continues to grab market share from its competitors and now has a higher market share than Toyota, Nissan, or Honda in all major global markets except the US and Japan.[17] Even in the highly competitive US market, its market share surpassed 10 percent in 2011.[18]

The company's rapid international growth and localization was achieved by transferring its domestic production system, which has become very advanced and sophisticated, to other countries with only minor modifications. In contrast to the lean production system of Japanese automobile makers, which relies heavily on highly skilled production workers, Hyundai's production system, while incorporating some Japanese features, is primarily driven by engineer-led automation with more standardized labor processes. As a consequence, it is much less vulnerable to a lack of training or understanding by workers and has been introduced in other countries with relatively little difficulty as the company needed to invest only moderately into the training of its local workforces. Moreover, the company carefully chose international locations that offered relatively high flexibility in terms of employee work schedules as well as adjustments of workforces in response to market demand. Even in advanced Western countries, it found locations with relatively flexible labor markets, such as the Southern states of the US, and countries in Central Eastern Europe. As a result, unlike its Japanese competitors, after starting production in its international manufacturing plants Hyundai achieved productivity levels matching or even surpassing that of its Korean factories within a few years.[19]

Taken together, Hyundai Motor transformed itself from a second tier automobile manufacturer, which relied heavily on its domestic production base, to a leading global player with localized operations in all major markets. It achieved this through its aggressive international expansion and the relative ease with which its competitive advantage in manufacturing could be transferred to other countries.

LG Electronics

Whereas LG Electronics has been a leading manufacturer of electronic appliances in Korea for several decades, as described in Chapters 3 and 4, its international recognition was still fairly low in the 1990s. Moreover, in contrast to Samsung Electronics, it did not have a globally leading market position in even a single product line. The company was perceived as clearly lagging behind the best Japanese and Western competitors in terms of technology, productivity, and globalization.

However, this situation did not deter LG Electronics from making bold investments to strengthen its competitiveness. On the technology side, it sought external help when necessary. Its alliance with, and later on the takeover of, Zenith, a leading American digital display technology company, helped it with acquiring critical patents. At the same time, it took advantage of the technological paradigm shift from analog to digital technology by aggressively investing into digital display technology and production. Thereby, LG managed to take the lead from Japanese producers who had difficulties with shifting their resources from analog to digital technology.[20]

At the same time, LG rapidly ramped up its production network in the late 1990s over the whole globe, resulting in a total number of thirty-one overseas production sites by 2000. It also quickly extended its international R&D and sales networks to seventeen and forty-five subsidiaries, respectively, by 2007.[21] The company did not always stick to full ownership when expanding globally and flexibly entered joint ventures when necessary, particularly in emerging markets in Asia.[22] However, it took great care in integrating its international sites, particularly in manufacturing. Similarly to Samsung, it also took its main group-internal suppliers, such as LG Display, LG Innotech, and LG Communications to its international locations to ensure it could establish a stable supply chain outside Korea. Moreover, it transferred various state-of-the-art operations management practices, such as modular manufacturing, from Korea to its overseas sites and thereby quickly achieved high productivity. The company also quickly introduced an integrated purchasing and supply chain management system across all its global sites and thereby made further efficiency gains.[23]

While pushing for integration and efficiency gains in its supply chain and manufacturing operations, LG showed a high flexibility in its sales and marketing efforts to satisfy customer needs in each country and region. After studying local preferences intensively, it developed customized solutions that often gave it a strong advantage over competitors.[24]

Overall, the company has pursued a strategy of rapid and comprehensive globalization since the late 1990s. This strategy was supported by strong integration efforts in supply chain and operations management and equally strong localization and customization efforts in product development and marketing. Recently, LG Electronics has been pre-empting its major competitors in new markets. For example, it ramped up its local presence in Nigeria and built a major customer service center in Lagos in 2008.[25]

There is no doubt that LG's boldness and flexibility has been met with great success. It has become the world's second largest producer of flat panel TV sets and the third largest manufacturer of mobile phones. Its revenues are well balanced across all regions of the world, and approximately two thirds of its total workforce is located outside Korea. It has also become a well known brand across the globe.[26]

Venture Tigers

Aside from the large business groups, numerous independent venture firms have been founded in Korea, particularly since the 1990s. As these companies are younger and smaller than their *chaebol* counterparts, most of them are not as well known yet outside their home country. However, many of these firms have become strong international competitors in their industries throughout the last decade. Subsequently, a few among them are introduced.

Humax

Humax is a producer of digital set-top boxes (devices that connect TV sets with external signals). The company was founded in 1989 by seven engineering graduates from Seoul National University led by Byun Dae-gyu, the company's current CEO.[27]

Initially, the company manufactured image processing boards for PCs, but shifted its business to home karaoke machines, video CD players, and eventually to digital set-top boxes when it sensed the soaring demand in this market. It always developed its own products and sold them under its own brand. Moreover, Humax rapidly internationalized its business. It started exporting its products a few years after its establishment and opened its first overseas manufacturing facility in Northern Ireland in 1997. Additional overseas subsidiaries quickly followed.[28]

Currently, Humax has ten subsidiaries outside Korea, including manufacturing sites in Poland, India, and Thailand and sales offices all around the world. International sales account for the overwhelming proportion of the company's total business.[29]

Taken together, Humax has not only quickly established itself as an independent producer of hardware and software in a variety of markets, but also become a strong international competitor with fully globalized operations. The company achieved this through the entrepreneurial spirit of its founders who combined strong engineering capabilities with a sense for market trends and the willingness to invest boldly into global expansion.

AhnLab

AhnLab was founded in 1995 by Ahn Cheol-soo, a medical doctor. When his computer was infected by a software virus, he wrote a program to remove it. He called this anti-virus program "vaccine" and subsequently started a business by selling it to others. Although he retired as chairman in 2005, the company still carries his name.[30]

Soon after its foundation, AhnLab quickly became a leading supplier of virus protection software. As the demand for such software exploded on account of the rapid proliferation of the Internet, the company grew quickly and is now the dominant Internet security provider in Korea.

AhnLab is famous in Korea, but it also has research and sales operations in more than twenty countries worldwide.[31] While most revenues are currently still generated in Korea, the company intends to expand its international business by focusing more on web security services that combine analysis and treatment of network problems.[32] Overall, AhnLab is another example of a thriving venture firm which grew from humble beginnings through a combination of innovative ideas, entrepreneurial spirit, bold business strategy, and fast implementation.

NCsoft

NCsoft was founded in 1997 by Kim Tack-jin who previously worked at Hyundai Electronics' R&D center. Initially, the company developed enterprise software, but quickly shifted its focus to massive multiplayer online games that allow thousands of players to participate simultaneously over the Internet. In 1998, the company landed a hit with its "Lineage" game which attracted great attention in Korea's rapidly growing online game community.[33]

After this initial success, NCsoft swiftly went global. Beginning in 2000, it set up subsidiaries or joint ventures in the US, Europe, Japan, Taiwan, and Thailand. Most importantly, it also globalized its development activities. The company works with three development studios in the US, which collaborate with its domestic developers. Some of its games are targeted at East Asian markets, whereas others are released first in Western countries.[34]

As of 2010, approximately two thirds of the company's sales are still from within Korea. However, NCsoft has firmly established itself as a global game developing company and made international operations a main pillar of its business.[35] The company achieved this by capitalizing on its development competencies and going international without hesitation.

SM Entertainment

SM Entertainment focuses on the business of music entertainment, particularly pop and dance performances targeted at young audiences. It was founded in 1995 by Lee Soo-man, who was formerly a singer. The company searches for young talents, hires them, trains them extensively, and then promotes them either as bands or solo performers.[36]

Only a few years after establishing itself in the Korean entertainment industry, SM went international by promoting its singers and dancers outside its home country. It created a joint venture in Japan and recently another one in Thailand with a local media company. The company also has a subsidiary in the US. Throughout the last decade, it capitalized on the rising worldwide interest in Korean entertainment symbolized by the "*hallyu*" wave and succeeded in organizing numerous concerts and events of its performers around the world.

However, the company does not only send its Korean singers and bands to other countries. Since 2006, it has also conducted regular global auditions to recruit talents in other countries.[37] In other words, it is exporting its business model of early talent recruiting, extensive training, and professional promotion. The company is another example of the successful implementation of Tiger Management. It expands aggressively and seizes business opportunities around the world relentlessly.

Conclusion

In this chapter, it has been shown that Korean companies, after being held back by the post-1997 financial crisis for a few years, staged a major comeback in the twenty-first century. They emerged from the crisis with streamlined operations which reinforced their competitiveness and enabled them to start growing again on a sounder financial base. They steeply increased their international business both through exports and through foreign direct investment, while maintaining a high profitability and keeping their debt at a low level.

Large *chaebol* tigers rapidly expanded their business around the globe. In particular, they invested heavily in emerging countries of the Asia Pacific region, such as China, India, and ASEAN (Association of Southeast Asian Nations) countries. At the same time, they also increasingly penetrated regions where they did not have much of a presence before, such as Latin America and Africa. As a result, they have built up significant market shares in all regions of the world.

At the same time, many Korean venture tigers also established themselves as strong competitors. From humble beginnings, they developed very competitive products and services, often in new industries. When given an opportunity, they aggressively scaled up their operations not only in Korea, but also in other countries.

In short, Korean companies of all types (old and new, large and small) continue to strengthen their presence on the world markets. They have refined Tiger Management and addressed problems such as over-indebtedness and weak corporate governance. At the same time, they have kept the essence of Tiger Management: making relentless efforts, seizing opportunities whenever they emerge, and implementing their strategies with very high speed and flexibility.

Notwithstanding their impressive performance throughout the last decade, some caution seems warranted regarding large *chaebols*, however. The total number of subsidiaries of the thirty largest Korean business groups has more than doubled from 500 in 2006 to 1,087 in 2011.[38] This documents the groups' fast growth, but also raises some concerns about the soundness and sustainability of their expansion, particularly when considering that many of the newly added subsidiaries have posted losses. After all, diversification into new industries only appears to make sense in the globally competitive business environment of the twenty-first century when good synergies with pre-existing activities can be realized, and there are doubts regarding this synergy potential in some cases. As the *chaebols*' financial position is now much healthier than before the Asian financial crisis, their risk of falling back into serious trouble is greatly reduced even if they should fail with some of their investments. Nonetheless, there is a possibility that some *chaebols* may be over-reaching again, and another shakeout in the future cannot be ruled out in the event of another economic crisis.

Part III

Cornerstones of Tiger Management

7 Tiger strategy

How Korean companies compete

Our DNA at Samsung is now: winning in all segments, winning in all markets.
A Samsung Electronics manager, commenting
on his company's mobile phone business[1]

Over the last several decades, Korean companies have achieved an almost miraculous performance. They seemingly came from nowhere to become leading global competitors in many industries. They develop ever new technologies, create ever new products and services, and find ever new markets in which to sell them.

In this chapter, Korean companies' strategic management will be discussed as the first cornerstone of Tiger Management. Generally speaking, firms need to have a basic strategic orientation that guides their long-term plans and decisions. Moreover, they also need to have mechanisms that enable them to implement their strategies. As will be shown, Tiger strategy consists of three basic elements: growth orientation, speed, and flexibility. Korean companies' basic orientation is growth seeking, and speed and flexibility are the guiding principles for implementing strategies.

Strategic orientation: growth, growth, growth

When managers give their companies a strategic orientation, they must weigh business opportunities against business risks. Should they endeavor into new activities to take advantage of opportunities, or should they rather consolidate their business to control the risks? Regarding this fundamental question, Korean managers and entrepreneurs tend to focus strongly on new business opportunities, even if the pursuit of these opportunities comes with significant risks. They are boldly seeking growth for their companies in three ways: adding new products and services, developing new technologies, and seeking new markets.

New products and services

As already discussed in the previous chapters, Korean companies and business groups are famous for their high diversification and wide portfolio of business interests. Tables 3.1 to 3.5 provide an overview of the development of the largest five *chaebols* over the last fifty years. The data show that they continuously added member firms and expanded into ever new manufacturing and service industries. As a result of this expansion, the groups experienced an explosive growth in their sales and employees over time. In other words, the *chaebols* have grown so quickly because they have continuously seized new opportunities to widen their portfolio of business interests by offering new products and services to their customers.

There is a widespread view that much of the *chaebols'* growth and diversification is not the result of genuine managerial decisions, but rather induced by the Korean government, which has guided the investment decisions of business groups particularly in the 1960s and 1970s. Whereas the important role of the government during the early stage of Korea's industrialization cannot be denied, this view needs to be qualified in two ways.

First, as discussed in Chapter 3, notwithstanding all the governmental guidance and support, investment decisions still needed to be made by company executives, not government officials. Given the limited human, financial, and technological resources the groups commanded at that time, these decisions were bold and must sometimes have been regarded as reckless by contemporary observers. For example, how could anyone assume in the 1960s that Hyundai could not only enter, but actually thrive in the automobile manufacturing business? Who had expected Samsung to manage a successful entry into the semiconductor industry in the 1970s?

Second, as can be seen from Tables 3.1 to 3.5, a large part of the *chaebols'* growth and diversification actually took place since the 1980s, a period when the governmental influence on the business sector had receded. In other words, many decisions to expand into new products and services have been genuinely made by the business leaders themselves without external interference.

The strong growth through aggressive product diversification is not a unique feature of the largest *chaebols*, but is also common among smaller business groups and among Korean companies in general. For example, Lotte Group started in 1950 as a beverage producer and now has fifty-six group companies in industries as diverse as food and beverage, logistics, tourism, chemicals, construction, machinery, and financial services.[2] Hanwha Group originates from an explosives business, which was founded in 1952, and now has forty-four member firms in the chemical, engineering and construction, insurance, securities, retailing, and tourism industries.[3] Kumho Asiana Group has its origins in a taxi company established in Gwangju in 1946 and now has sixteen group companies engaged in the chemical, tire, bus and air transportation, logistics, and construction industries.[4] The list of such examples could be easily extended.

New technologies

Korean companies and business groups do not only enlarge themselves by extending the scope of their activities into new industries. They also seek growth by aggressively developing new technologies, which help them in turn to create new products and services.

On an aggregated level, this can be most easily seen by international data on companies' research and development (R&D) investments. As of 2008, Korean companies invested 3.77 percent of their value added and 2.53 percent of the national GDP into R&D. These ratios are the highest and second highest (behind Japan) among the world's large economies, far higher than those of their counterparts in leading Western countries such as the US and Germany.[5] In other words, Korean firms are heavily investing into the development of new technologies.

R&D investments are inevitably very risky, as there is a lot of technological uncertainty as well as market uncertainty when developing new technologies. However, the Korean companies' technological output has also rapidly increased in recent years. The country's world share of "triadic patent families" (sets of patents which are filed in the US, the EU, and Japan) has almost increased five-fold between 1995 and 2009, from 0.92 percent to 4.17 percent.[6] This indicates that the Korean firms as a whole are gaining high returns on their investment into new technologies.

Similar observations can be made for specific companies and industries. Soon after entering the electronic industry, firms such as Samsung or LG, not satisfied with the perspective of producing only under licenses provided by foreign producers, went all out to accumulate stronger engineering and R&D capabilities. Often, reverse engineering (i.e. the decomposing of products manufactured by other firms to understand the technologies they are built on) served as a starting point to gain an initial understanding of related technologies. Then, huge task forces of engineers and researchers were set up who often worked around the clock in order to create first prototypes of their own products within short time limits. After extremely intensive engineering efforts and many trials and errors, these prototypes were moved into mass production, thus enabling the companies to compete globally with their own products and technologies. This pattern of technological catch-up by dedicating huge resources to technological development was repeated for many electronic products, such as TV sets, microwave ovens, and flat panel displays.[7]

However, Korean firms are by no means satisfied with just catching up techno-logically with foreign rivals. They continue investing heavily into R&D and strive for technological leadership whenever possible. In many cases, such as Samsung in memory chips or Samsung and LG in flat panel displays, they succeeded.

Another aspect that documents the companies' strong determination to enhance their growth by acquiring ever more technologies is the aggressive expansion of their R&D organizations. An extreme example is that of Samsung Electronics, where about 30 percent of all employees belong to the R&D workforce.[8] More generally, the companies' R&D is now reaching out both geographically and technologically in order to find new sources of growth in the future. Many large firms have set up international R&D networks, which they are steadily extending. Samsung operates sixteen R&D centers outside Korea in eight different coun-tries,[9] whereas LG Electronics has thirty laboratories around the world.[10] At the same time, they are continuously looking for new technological opportunities. For example, LG Electronics is recently investing into solar battery technology[11] and Hyundai Motor into hybrid and electric cars.[12]

In short, Korean companies seek new growth not only by aggressive expansion into new products and services, but also by investing heavily into the develop-ment of new technologies. They do not shy away from the high risk and the inev-itable failures of R&D efforts. Their persistent determination to create ever more and better technologies has overall proved to be very successful.

New markets

Aside from a strong drive to diversify into new products and services, and to develop new technologies, another aspect of Korean companies' growth orienta-tion is their dynamic penetration of new geographic markets. Their early and bold advancement into many countries and regions has already been discussed in Chapters 4 and 6.

It is noteworthy that Korean companies often take major risks when advancing into new regions. This high risk tolerance covers two aspects: the internal risk that the company may not have sufficient resources to sustain its activities in new markets and the external country-specific risk. The internal risk was particularly prevalent during the early stages of international expansion, when Korean compa-nies had barely any overseas business experience and little knowledge of how to organize international activities. These internal limitations did not deter them from advancing boldly into unknown territories. Not surprisingly, they experi-enced various failures. These failures, however, provided the companies with valuable lessons on how to improve their international market expansion efforts. For example, as discussed in Chapter 4, Hyundai Construction capitalized on its early experiences with road construction in Thailand in the 1960s when advancing shortly thereafter into Vietnam or Middle East countries. Hyundai Motor had to close its first overseas factory in Canada in 1994 due to insufficient local demand. This experience gave the company invaluable lessons when it built a global production network thereafter, as shown in Chapter 6.

The companies' high tolerance of external country-specific risks can be seen through their early and aggressive investments into developing and emerging countries, which were often shunned by competitors (see Chapter 4). While some of these investments were inevitably lost because of economic or political instability in target countries, the companies' risk taking approach, nonetheless, was rewarding overall for two reasons. First, as the Korean firms moved into markets which were avoided by other companies, they could often reap higher returns on account of less competition. Second, as the companies' experience in developing and emerging countries accumulated over time, they became experts in operating in such markets with unstable environments, which in turn proved to become a genuine advantage when competing with other multinational firms in emerging markets later on.

The Korean companies' drive to move aggressively into such "frontier markets" is still undaunted. For example, LG Electronics recently scaled up its business in various African countries, such as Nigeria, Senegal, and Angola.[13]

Strategy implementation: speed and flexibility

Whereas the strategic orientation of Korean companies is strongly focused on growth, the implementation of their strategies is guided by high amounts of speed and flexibility. In other words, Korean firms implement their strategies very quickly, and they do not limit their implementation methods to specific approaches and policies. Instead, in each context and situation, they pragmatically choose whatever appears to be the most promising way to achieve their goals. This flexibility has two aspects: external flexibility in the selection of products, methods of technology acquisition, and markets, and internal flexibility regarding how business activities can be supported from within a company or business group.

Speed

High implementation speed is a signature feature of Korean companies, as symbolized by the phrase *"palli palli"* (quickly quickly). It is simply regarded as normal in Korea to do things very quickly since the country's rapid industrialization in the 1960s and 1970s.

Various examples of high-speed implementation by Korean firms have already been discussed in the preceding chapters. Hyundai Motor entered the automobile business from the scratch in 1967 and started assembling cars only one year later.[14] Hyundai Heavy Industries began constructing its Ulsan shipyard in 1972 and delivered its first two ships in 1974.[15] Samsung Electronics created a task force in 1982 to enter the very large scale integrated circuit (VLSI) business and succeeded in producing them in 1984 after building a manufacturing site within only six months.[16] In other words, Korean firms have been repeatedly breaking the conventional wisdom of how long it takes in capital- and knowledge-intensive industries to build a facility, to develop a product or to enter a market. Their extremely high implementation speed often constitutes a major competitive advantage, particularly in high tech industries.[17]

How can Korean firms implement their strategies so quickly? Part of the response lies in the leadership style of Korean executives and the attitude of their employees, which will be discussed in greater detail in Chapters 8 and 9. Senior executives have almost absolute authority in their companies. Therefore, no time needs to be spent on persuading all subordinated managers and employees about the validity and importance of managerial directions. Everybody will immediately focus on implementing them. Moreover, Korean workforces tend to be extremely motivated and work very intensively and for long hours, if needed. In fact, they often try to exceed preset targets and schedules.[18]

Furthermore, Korean companies have also developed a number of specific managerial tools which help them move faster.[19] For important work, they routinely set up task forces. When multiple implementation problems occur, they work on solving these problems simultaneously, not sequentially. Moreover, groups such as Samsung have also developed sophisticated internal knowledge transfer systems that enable them to increase their implementation speed further.

External flexibility

Korean companies showed a high flexibility in selecting their business activities from their early days. As discussed in Chapter 3, they jumped on whatever business opportunity was given to them when the government allocated import quotas or identified "strategic industries." For example, Samsung, initially a trade business, ventured into sugar and textiles in the 1950s, as these were lucrative industries in Korea at that time because of government intervention. In the 1960s and 1970s, it expanded into electronics, petrochemicals, machinery, and shipbuilding and thereby took full advantage of the government's industrial policies. Similar patterns can be observed for other *chaebols*. Later on, international market opportunities substituted government policies as growth drivers. In the 1980s, after having established itself in the consumer electronics sector, Samsung aggressively moved into microelectronics as Chairman Lee Byung-chull noticed that this industry has high long-term potential for growth and profits. Most recently, Samsung Group has identified environment-, energy- and health-related businesses as future growth sectors and is therefore focusing on LED displays, automobile batteries, solar batteries, medical instruments, and biopharmaceuticals in its business development.[20] Some of these industries are quite different from Samsung's current core businesses in electronics and microelectronics. All the same, the group heavily invests into these areas as it senses attractive future business opportunities in these fields.

A similar pragmatism is applied regarding the technology acquisition strategies of Korean companies. Whereas the selection of technologies they are focusing on is naturally guided by perceived future business opportunities, they are very flexible regarding the means by which these technologies are acquired. For example, Hyundai accumulated much of its initial knowledge on how to assemble cars through a licensing agreement with Ford that covered a comprehensive technology transfer by American engineers sent to Korea. After the partnership with Ford broke down five years later, Hyundai entered another licensing contract with Mitsubishi Motors, which granted the Korean side more autonomy. In the following year, the company hired George Turnbull, a former managing director of British Leyland, as vice president, who in turn recruited six senior European engineers to assist him building up engineering and design capabilities in the company. Only two years later, the company started the production of the first indigenous Korean car, the Pony.[21]

Similar patterns can be observed for other Korean companies. When LG entered the electronics industry in 1958, it hired an experienced German engineer who led the company's first efforts to assemble radios using foreign parts after having reverse engineered Japanese products. At the same time, crucial engineering knowledge was transferred from the German engineer to his Korean colleagues. However, these skills proved insufficient when the company moved to the assembly of TV sets in the 1960s. Therefore, the company entered into a licensing agreement with Hitachi, which included intensive technical training of LG engineers who were sent to Japan. These efforts eventually enabled LG to develop and manufacture its own products.[22] In the 1990s, when LG Electronics entered the digital display industry, it created a joint venture with Philips and took over Zenith, a US company, to strengthen its technological competencies in this field.[23]

Whereas the specific methods of technological learning are somewhat different between the automobile industry and the electronic industry, the bottom line is much the same for the two examples: the companies did not rely on a specific method or a specific partner when acquiring crucial technologies. Instead, they flexibly chose those technology acquisition methods that looked most promising to achieve their goals at each stage, and selected those partners who appeared most suitable.

Finally, Korean companies also show much flexibility when entering new markets. When they started internationalizing, they simply targeted those countries where they could find customers. Hyundai Construction initiated its overseas business in countries such as Thailand, Vietnam, Guam, and Papua New Guinea.[24] Quite famously, the first exports of Hyundai Motor's Pony were shipped to Ecuador.[25]

Later on in the 1980s, having developed globally competitive products and having gained some international business expertise, Korean companies focused more on developed markets in North America and Europe, as these regions were most attractive on account of their high volumes and price levels. Since the 1990s, however, they have primarily expanded again in emerging markets such as China, India, or the ASEAN countries. The reason for this temporal sequence of attention on where to do business is straightforward: the companies focus on those countries and regions that are most attractive at a given point of time. Korean firms do not dismiss any place in the world for doing business. They go anywhere when they perceive a good opportunity or market potential.

Internal flexibility

Korean companies are not only flexible when choosing the products and services they produce and sell, the means by which they acquire new technologies, and the countries and regions that they enter and penetrate, but also regarding their internal resource allocation when they implement their growth strategies. This internal flexibility applies to the use of various resources, such as capital, knowledge, and manpower.

Fundamentally, commonly available resources such as patents, brands, and management tools are freely shared in Korean companies and business groups.[26] This free internal resource sharing may result in significant benefits for each member company or business unit, such as when it is associated with a well-known brand.

However, the internal flexibility of Korean firms and groups does not end with such general resource sharing. Instead, it is extended to the discretionary shifting of internal resources according to the needs of specific business units. In other words, capital and human resources are flexibly allocated to those business activities that need them most at a given point of time.

A typical situation where such internal resource shifting occurs is when a company or business group enters a new industry or a new market. In such cases, the new venture is backed up through the transfer of capital and skilled managerial

and technical staff from other internal units. Such massive internal
often crucial for the success of new market or industry entries, part
Korean companies tend to diversify aggressively into new businesses th
always familiar with. For example, the diversification of Hyundai into
mobile industry or that of Samsung into the semiconductor industry woul
have been viable without such massive internal support.

Conclusion

In this chapter, the three main features of Tiger strategy have been reviewed: growth
orientation, speed, and flexibility. Korean companies always seek new business
opportunities and therefore aggressively invest into new industries, acquire new
technologies, and enter new markets. They are not afraid of potential failures when
doing so, as they focus on opportunities rather than risks and even capitalize on
miscarriages, which offer valuable experiences and lessons for the future.

Moreover, the companies implement their strategies with a very high speed.
Once strategic directions are decided on, all involved managers and workers
exclusively focus on making them reality. Swift implementation is supported by
multiple task forces that solve problems simultaneously when needed. At the
same time, Korean companies are highly flexible in the implementation of their
growth strategies. They choose new fields of activity, develop new technologies,
and enter new markets whenever they look promising and are not selective about
the means to achieve their goals. In short: doing anything with anybody and anywhere is fine as long as this results in new revenues and profits. Additionally,
resources are flexibly shifted within companies and business groups to those areas
that need such support at any given point of time.

Taken together, we can see that the virtues of Tiger Management can be clearly
identified in the strategy of Korean companies. They show boldness and perseverance when formulating their strategies, and speed and flexibility when they
implement them. At the same time, these components of Tiger strategy are complementing each other. On the one hand, the companies' bold growth orientation
facilitates speed and flexibility, as there will be little resistance to such flexible
approaches as long as the business as a whole is growing and performing well. On
the other hand, speed and flexibility support aggressive growth strategies as they
give the companies a wide range of choices to achieve their goals. In combination,
growth orientation, speed, and flexibility have made Korean companies fierce
competitors in a wide range of industries around the world. Their performance can
therefore be expected to remain strong in the foreseeable future as long as their
diversification is supported by reasonable synergies and they do not overstretch
their resources again, as some of them did in the 1990s.

8 Tiger leadership

How Korean executives lead their companies

The idea that if someone has become a business leader, he can have a more convenient or fancier life than other people or has the chance to enjoy ever bigger pleasures or satisfactions is wrong. Rather, he needs to use his position as a happy opportunity to do something for other people.

Kim Woo-choong[1]

Change everything except your wife and children.

Lee Kun-hee, to his employees[2]

In this chapter, another cornerstone of Tiger Management will be discussed: Tiger leadership. Anywhere in the world, corporate executives need to display leadership in order to motivate their subordinates, and to maintain and strengthen the cohesiveness of their companies' organizations. In other words, leadership is a crucial and universal task for business managers.

As will be shown, however, Korean companies' owners and executives have developed a specific leadership style, which lends their companies great dynamism and induces managers and workers to make outstanding efforts in order to achieve corporate goals. Tiger leadership consists of four basic elements that mutually support each other: charisma, corporate values, ambitious goal setting, and crisis creation. In combination, these leadership features create organizations that continuously strive to become ever stronger and better. They never rest, as when one goal is achieved and one challenge is met, they will immediately move on to the next. It will also be shown that Tiger leadership is supported by three underlying common traits of Korean companies: centralization of managerial authority, planning and control support by chairmen's planning offices, and strong intra-organizational coherence.

The leadership style of Korean executives

Leadership by charisma

One common feature of many Korean business leaders is their strong charisma. They are capable of creating enthusiasm and loyalty among others, particularly the management and workforce of a company. Charisma is commonly perceived as an individual trait. However, observers have frequently noted that charismatic leadership is in fact very widespread among the owners and executives of Korean firms,[3] with Hyundai founder Chung Ju-yung, Samsung founder Lee Byung-chull, and Daewoo founder Kim Woo-choong being particularly famous examples.

What constitutes the charisma of Korean business leaders? One important feature of their leadership is the ability to create compelling visions and communicate them effectively. For example, former Samsung chairman Lee Byung-chull, when venturing into the semiconductor industry, inspired his subordinates by likening computer chips to the "rice of the industry" which he predicted to become a backbone of industrial innovation in the twenty-first century.[4] This illustration proved to be very powerful, as it conveyed the vision that the company would become a major player in future industries in a way which was easy to understand for Koreans.

Whereas such inspiring messages are an important part of Korean business leaders' charisma, they are complemented by another crucial aspect: leadership by providing a role model. Korean executives expect their subordinates to work long hours and dedicate everything they have to do the best possible job. Though the Confucian work ethic also contributes to the willingness of staff members to devote themselves to their companies, such dedication to work is strongest when they can observe that their senior leaders are working particularly hard. Hyundai founder, Chung Ju-yung, was an outstanding example of such leadership by good example. For instance, when Hyundai Construction built Korea's first highway between Seoul and Busan in the late 1960s, Chairman Chung worked day and night on the construction site and slept only occasionally in an old company jeep. This behavior and attitude induced many other managers and workers to follow his example.[5] Daewoo chairman, Kim Woo-choong, was another business leader known for working extremely hard, thereby inspiring others to do the same and creating a strong entrepreneurial spirit in the entire business group. He regularly worked for 100 hours every week and did not take a single day off in the first twenty years after starting his business, except on the morning of his daughter's wedding ceremony.[6]

Taken together, Korean business leaders gain their charisma from inspiring communication, which is, however, critically complemented by setting outstanding examples in terms of work attitude and efforts. Their actual behavior gives credibility to their visions and messages, as others can observe that these visions are not empty words, but have to be taken seriously and are followed through by actions of the leaders themselves.

Leadership by corporate values

Corporate values represent another aspect of how the chairmen of Korean companies lead their organizations. These values are mostly shown by company mottos or slogans (*sahoon*, in Korean) which indicate what the company and its employees should fundamentally aim for. While such company mottos are not a specifically Korean phenomenon, they represent, more so than in other countries, the personal values of the group chairman or company leader in Korea.[7] Moreover, they do not exclusively focus on how external stakeholders, such as customers, should be approached, but are in large part directed at the behavior and attitudes of company employees among themselves.[8]

Table 8.1 shows the current core values of the ten largest business groups. As can be seen from this list, there is a considerable variety regarding their contents. Many groups focus on modern values such as "respect for people." At the same time, some groups emphasize more traditional values such as "passion" or

Table 8.1 Core values of Korea's ten largest business groups, 2011

Business group	Core values
Samsung	People first, striving for excellence, leading change, integrity management, co-prosperity
Hyundai Motor	Challenging action, communication and collaboration, customers first, global mindset, respect for people
SK	Passion, love, challenge, innovation, integrity, responsibility
LG	Creating value for customers, respecting people
Lotte	Customer orientation, originality, collaboration, responsibility, passion
POSCO	Customer orientation, pursuit of challenges, implementation focus, respecting people, moral integrity
Hyundai Heavy Industries	Imagination without limit, search for challenges, value creation, keeping promises, respecting people
GS	Dreaming of tomorrow together with customers, creating new values in life
Hanjin	Value innovation, relationship innovation, system innovation, capability innovation
Hanwha	Challenge, integrity, dedication

Source: Company websites.

"dedication." As the values are direct reflections of the current chairmen's beliefs, they tend to be adjusted when the management control is handed over from one generation to the next.

Company mottos are quite important for corporate leadership in Korea because they do not only constitute statements of what leaders regard as important, but also have significant consequences for the internal cultures of groups and companies.[9] All members of an organization are expected to pursue these values in their daily professional activities. The companies also make serious efforts to instill them in their employees through systematic training programs, which will be discussed in more detail in Chapter 9. In short, Korean business leaders instrumentalize their personal values and beliefs by spelling them out in company mottos, and thereby giving their organizations fundamental directions regarding what is important and what should be emphasized in business activities.

Leadership by goal setting

Another important aspect of Tiger leadership is goal setting. Korean executives motivate their subordinates to work hard by setting very ambitious goals. At the same time, these goals are mostly very clear-cut.[10] For example, they may set the target that their company becomes the largest one in Korea in their industry within the next three years or one of the three top global companies within the next five years. Or they may set the goal of reaching a specific market share in a given country or market segment within a given number of months or years. Typically, the goals are directed at breaking past records or beating competitors.[11] As discussed in Chapter 2, setting concrete and ambitious goals has become customary in Korean companies since the country's rapid industrialization in the 1960s and 1970s.

For example, when Samsung Electronics advanced into the semiconductor business, Chairman Lee Byung-chull set the clear target of creating a working production line for 64K DRAM chips within six months.[12] He did so because he saw the boom in the semiconductor industry at that time, but also knew that his company needed to hurry up to enter the market before the demand fell off again. The engineering team fully achieved the target set by the chairman. Soon thereafter, Samsung started producing memory chips and thereby reduced the technological gap with leading competitors in the US and Japan from ten to four years. A few years later, the gap had totally disappeared.[13]

Goal setting in general has become widespread in Korean companies at all organizational levels. It is implemented by using "Management by Objectives" (MBO) as a tool to give managers clearly defined goals which they should fulfill within a given time limit.[14]

Setting bold goals can be a powerful motivation tool, as they are easy to verify and at the same time worthwhile to go for. Fulfilling them will constitute a major accomplishment for the whole company and its employees. However, this ambitious goal setting is only effective if the employees of a company actually believe that the goal is feasible. Otherwise, it could actually have negative effects on the morale of employees. They may become demotivated when they feel that they are being given unrealistic goals that cannot be achieved. Therefore, charismatic leadership is an important complement of ambitious goal setting, as business leaders must persuade their subordinates that the bold objectives are really feasible. At the same time, ambitious goal setting has often been combined with the fourth component of Tiger leadership: crisis creation.

Succession planning

Leadership by crisis creation

It is well known that in general, companies' managers and workers tend to make extraordinary efforts when being confronted with a crisis. A common perception that the whole company may go bankrupt and fall apart unless certain goals are met or certain situations are averted often results in heroic efforts. Routine procedures are substituted by an innovative search for new solutions. As a result, companies that overcome a crisis are often much more competitive when compared with the pre-crisis situation.

Normally, crises are regarded as a phenomenon coming from outside. For example, there may be a sudden change in customer demands, a big technological change that forces companies to innovate, or a supply shock, as during the oil crises. Korean business leaders, however, sometimes deliberatively create crises from *inside* their companies to push their organizations into extraordinary performances when coping with them.

For example, crisis creation played a major role in Hyundai Motor's breathtaking transformation from a small contract manufacturer of foreign cars into a world-class competitor. At each stage of its development, Hyundai's leaders created an internal crisis to maximize the company's performance.[15] First, they set an extremely short deadline for completing the first assembly plant. Next, the company's engineers were confronted with the even more challenging task of building a much larger factory, this time to produce indigenous Korean cars. A few years later, Hyundai's management decided to triple the production capacity again and to develop larger and technologically more advanced models, thereby exposing the whole company to another crisis to achieve these goals. Finally, the licensing contract with Mitsubishi Motors for engine technology was terminated, effectively forcing Hyundai's developers to create their own engines within a short period of time to ensure the company's survival. It should be noted that, whereas in retrospect the company's development looks very logical and natural, the challenges the leaders confronted the workforce with created a real crisis at each stage, as it had to be assumed that the company may fail if the goals were not achieved. In other words, the top management made a series of bold decisions, and the whole organization then had to scramble to justify these decisions.

Samsung Electronics is another company that has quickly leapt to ever higher levels of competitiveness through leadership by crisis creation. In the 1980s, following Chairman Lee Byung-chull's decision to enter the semiconductor industry, he repeatedly created a crisis management mode in his company by setting up two different development teams, one in Korea and one in the US, and asking them to work separately on specific technical solutions within an extremely short time frame. The two teams competed and, at the same time, collaborated with each other at each stage, resulting in technological advances which were much faster than those of American or Japanese competitors. Later on, when the company faced new technological challenges, a similar approach was frequently applied to overcome them: task forces were set up and ordered to find solutions within a very short time frame. Every time, the teams mastered the challenges given to them and delivered on time.[16]

Samsung's current chairman, Lee Kun-hee, also relies on leadership by creating a sense of crisis in the company. A few years after assuming managerial responsibility, he declared a "New Management" which focuses on quality. Two years later, large numbers of mobile phones of allegedly low quality were destroyed at a factory in front of the workforce.[17] The company's mobile phone division was given an ultimatum to produce phones of a quality comparable with leading global competitors within one year – otherwise the company would disengage from the industry. It took them only six months.[18]

In the following years, Samsung further moved up the ranks in the global electronics industry and has now become widely envied by competitors for its performance. However, Chairman Lee shocked his employees again by declaring in 2010 that "there is a real crisis now" and that "most of the company's flagship products and businesses will become obsolete within 10 years."[19] His communication style has been labeled as "3S" leadership: short, surprising, and shocking.[20]

Underlying forces of Tiger leadership

Centralization of authority

One important underlying feature of Korean companies which supports leadership by charisma, corporate values, goal setting, and crisis creation is the strong concentration of managerial power at the top level. Typically, the centralization of authority is so strong that all strategic directions are set by a single person: the chairman of the company or business group. The executive board will merely approve the leader's directions.

An illustrative example of the high power distance between the chairman and other executive managers is the case of Hyundai's former chairman, Chung Ju-yung. It has been observed that his regular meetings with the presidents of major group companies served to give them the impression that the distance between him and them was as great as between them and new recruits.[21] Such extreme centralization of managerial power appears to have receded only gradually even in recent years. Samsung's current chairman, Lee Kun-hee's, leadership has sometimes been referred to as "emperor management," as he makes all major strategic decisions and has the power to promote, demote, hire, or fire other managers, regardless of their rank.[22]

One reason for this power concentration at the top level is the strong cultural influence of Confucianism in Korea discussed in Chapter 2. According to Confucian ethics, the father holds absolute authority in a family. All others have to follow his views and obey his orders. Therefore, it can be said that centralized top-down management by a single leader in each company or business group is natural in Korea from a cultural viewpoint. As mentioned in Chapter 2, family-like bonds and relationships are commonly emphasized and cultivated in Korean companies. Senior leaders are considered quasi-father figures.[23]

Moreover, beyond such cultural aspects, there is also an important institutional factor behind the centralized control of Korean companies: unity of ownership and management. Korean companies and business groups are not only managed by their chairmen, they are also owned by them. Even in large, diversified *chaebols*, complicated cross-shareholding structures are in place to make sure that all companies are controlled by the owner family and thereby, the group chairman.[24] As Korean businesses mostly have been founded and raised by individual entrepreneurs, who later on handed over control to their children, there are only relatively few companies in Korea where ownership and management are separated.[25] The common unification of ownership and management gives the chairmen even stronger control over their companies.

owner/manager

Chairmen's planning offices

Whereas the strong Confucian roots in the Korean culture, and the unity of ownership and management, give business leaders enormous power to display strong leadership, there is another important background factor that supports Tiger leadership: the support of chairmen by their personal planning offices.

All major Korean companies and business groups have such organizational units that report directly and exclusively to the chairmen. In large business groups, between 50 and 200 staff members work in these offices, which thereby have a considerable size.[26] More importantly, they play a crucial role in the overall planning and control of companies and groups. As they are directly linked to the chairmen, and staffed by elite managers, they are regarded as "nerve centers" of the overall organization and have a very strong internal standing.[27] All other departments or group companies have to provide them with any information they request. This strong internal authority, combined with the analytical capabilities of their highly skilled staff members, allow the planning offices to support the chairmen through high quality analyses and insights which maximize the chances that the right directions will be set.

Moreover, the planning offices are also instrumental for the implementation of directions and policies set by business leaders. They are perceived as the organizational extension of the chairmen, and therefore have the authority and the means to watch the implementation of managerial directions in each department or group company closely. In other words, they increase the effectiveness of chairmen's policies by ensuring that they are implemented.

The planning offices are not just staff organizations that support the overall planning and control of Korean companies. They are also instrumental for the features of Tiger leadership discussed earlier in this chapter: charisma, corporate values, goal setting, and crisis creation. From the back stage, they greatly help Korean business leaders to gain important insights and make right decisions. As a consequence, the acceptance of leaders' decisions will be higher in their companies. The leaders themselves will be regarded as more charismatic, as they build up track records of setting the right directions for their companies. Managers and workers will work even harder to pursue corporate values, achieve the ambitious goals set by business leaders, and overcome the crises that have been created by them.

Strong intra-organizational coherence

A third underlying factor which supports the leadership style of Korean executives is the strong intra-organizational coherence which can be found in their companies. Similar to other East Asian countries, strong teamwork in groups and organizations is regarded as a cultural norm. There are two important concepts that support the internal coherence of companies and other organizations in Korea: "*jeong*" and "*inwha*."

Jeong can be roughly translated as "human affection." It represents the notion that people feel much more comfortable interacting with other people if they know them well. Although this preference is a general trait of human psychology, it is particularly strong in Korea. Notably, *jeong* basically builds up by getting used to each other, as company employees do with their colleagues they see every day. It does not necessarily mean that the individuals among whom *jeong* is created will like each other.[28] There may be personal aversions between colleagues because of differences in character or personal taste. Regardless of such aversions, they still get along and work together effectively, as they know each other well. In other words, *jeong* is quite robust against individual tensions and conflicts.

Inwha basically means "harmony." However, it particularly emphasizes harmony between individuals of unequal status and rank,[29] such as between supervisors and subordinates in companies, and can be linked to Confucian values which stress the cultivation of hierarchical relationships, as discussed in Chapter 2. As such, *inwha* implies that higher-ranked and senior people should be considerate towards lower-ranked individuals. In return, the lower-ranked person should follow the directions given by the higher-ranked counterpart and not destroy harmony by challenging him or her. Therefore, *inwha* helps smoothing vertical relationships in Korean companies.

Taken together, *jeong* and *inwha* represent much of the glue that holds together individual workers and managers in Korean companies. The existence of these mechanisms does not mean, however, that there are no serious tensions between colleagues working in the same company, department, or team. In fact, regardless of their cultural inclination for teamwork, Koreans simultaneously tend to have strong individual ambitions. For example, they are often personally determined to accumulate financial wealth or to move up quickly in a company hierarchy. In other words, strong individual aspirations and a strong team spirit tend to co-exist in Korean companies. This phenomenon may be described through the metaphor of "salad bowl groups" in which individuals mingle together but at the same time keep their personal interests.[30] Such co-existence of individual and collective ambitions can create considerable tensions and result in unproductive conflicts when not being dealt with properly.

This inherent tension between individual and collective agendas can, in fact, be best released and transformed into positive energy through strong leadership.[31] Highly ambitious corporate agendas, which are envisioned and credibly pursued by corporate leaders, give the workforces of Korean companies the impetus to work intensively together to meet both common and individual goals, as the latter will also tend to be fulfilled if a company has great success and can reward its employees generously. In this sense, the peculiar mix of strong individual ambitions and strong team spirit in Korean firms does not only support, but actually calls for strong leadership with bold corporate visions.

Conclusion

In this chapter, the specific features of Tiger leadership (charisma, corporate values, ambitious goal setting, and crisis creation) have been reviewed. It could be seen that these traits are vitally supported by the strong centralization of authority in Korean companies, by chairmen's planning offices which back business leaders from behind, and by the companies' strong intra-organizational coherence.

Apparently, not all Korean business executives have equal leadership capabilities. However, given the impressive performance of the country's companies and business groups over the last decades, it is also evident that overall, many chairmen have done an excellent job in leading their organizations to grow stronger and become ever more competitive.

Fundamentally, a virtuous circle between strong leadership and good performance has been established in many Korean companies. Through their charisma, values, goal setting, and crisis creation, business leaders have greatly increased the agility of their companies. Top level managerial directions, however bold and ambitious, have been implemented with outstanding speed and through enormous efforts of managers and workers. This speed often turned out to be a major competitive advantage for Korean companies, as their rivals from other countries could simply not match the pace by which the Koreans created new products and technologies and penetrated new markets. The strong performance of companies has in turn given additional legitimacy to Korean business leaders and their decisions. Their organizations do not just follow them because of the hierarchical Korean business culture, but also because they have built up a track record of good leadership over time.

Taken together, Tiger leadership is a cornerstone of Tiger Management that vitally contributes to the outstanding performance of many Korean companies. Business executives lead their organizations through charismatic communication, corporate values, ambitious goals setting, and crisis creation from within. The workforces of companies and business groups are working extremely hard to meet the targets and challenges given to them by the top management. As a result, Korean companies often move with a boldness, perseverance, speed, and agility unmatched by their competitors from other countris.

9 Recruiting, training, and rewarding Tiger employees

Korean style human resource management

> We respect the character and variety of human individuals. We regard our employees who are the source of value creation for customers as our most important asset.
>
> From LG Corporation's Corporate Vision[1]

Human resource management is the third and final cornerstone of Tiger Management. It is a crucial part of how Korean companies are managed overall. Without the tremendous efforts and dedication of their employees, and human resource management systems that make the best of their skills and capabilities, Korean companies would not have been able to travel as far as they have. They are keenly aware that, regardless of smart strategies and extraordinary leadership, a company's performance eventually relies on its employees' commitment and skills.

Korean companies' executives frequently emphasize that their managers and workers are their most valuable resource and asset.[2] Such proclamations are not empty words. In fact, the companies make extensive efforts to find, qualify, and motivate employees with true Tiger qualities: highly skilled and capable, strongly dedicated to their company, flexible and creative in their work, and never giving up.

Korean style human resource management rests on the specific way in which Korean firms recruit, train, and compensate their employees. The companies' specific approaches regarding these universally important functions of human resource management crucially contribute to their organizational dynamism. At the same time, there are some features of the Korean people in general which enable the companies to apply their peculiar human resource management systems: deep-seated hunger for economic success and exceptional education zeal.

How Korean companies manage their human resources

Korean companies have understood since their early days that in order to pursue their bold and aggressive business strategies successfully, they need to make the best possible use of their human talent. Therefore, they have developed human resource management systems that could be briefly described as follows: hire only highly qualified and motivated employees, develop their skills and capabilities as much as possible, and give them strong incentives to devote themselves fully to their work. These aspects of Korean style human resource management will be reviewed one by one.

Recruiting Tiger employees

From the beginning of their explosive growth in the 1960s, Korean companies needed to recruit workers and managers in large numbers to pursue their growth-oriented business strategies. In the early stages of expansion, the hiring process was often relatively informal, as the companies were still in the process of establishing their management systems. In these early days, the relationship-based recruiting of new employees was a frequent phenomenon.[3] Managers invited people with whom they had family ties, school ties (having attended the same high school or university), or regional ties (coming from the same home town or same region within Korea) to enter the company. The strong cultivation of such ties in the Korean society in general[4] resulted in this widespread practice. It can also be said that such "back door recruiting" was not necessarily a bad approach from the companies' viewpoint at the time, as there were social mechanisms in place which prevented it from just becoming cronyism. In East Asian countries such as Korea, the concept of "face" plays a major role in social interactions.[5] People lose face when their failures become known to other members of a group or organization, and such loss of face is regarded as a serious embarrassment. If someone hired by recommendation of another person does not perform well, this constitutes a loss of face for the recommending person as well as for the recruited person in the relationship with the recommender. As a consequence, in order not to lose face, managers would only recommend such people for hiring that they believed to be capable, and the recommended person would do his or her best in order not to embarrass the recommender. In this way, informal social mechanisms often worked as a reasonable substitute for a formal evaluation process of applicants when recruiting employees.

Subsequently, the recruitment process of large Korean firms became more formalized and sophisticated, particularly for managers and white-collar workers. As a result, from around the 1970s, applicants typically have to go through a selection process that consists of three stages: document screening, written tests and examinations, and personal interviews. At each stage, only the highest scoring applicants are selected for further consideration and advance to the next stage. Those applicants who have passed the third and final stage are still asked to take a physical examination, which they need to pass before they are eventually given a job offer.[6]

The overall selection process and its contents are summarized in Table 9.1. Certain evaluation aspects can sometimes overlap between the three stages. For example, a firm may consider external foreign language skill certifications in the screening of application documents before conducting its own foreign language test in the second stage.

Overall, it becomes clear that the selection process Korean companies apply when recruiting new employees is extensive and comprehensive. Almost any aspect of an applicant's background, capabilities, and personality one could think of is considered before a final evaluation is made. Whereas the overall structure of the process may have some similarities with those of firms from other countries that are also highly selective in their recruitment of new employees, there are some aspects which are particularly emphasized in Korea.

One such aspect is the age of the applicant, at least when new university graduates are recruited. However qualified an applicant, they may not be hired if they have passed a certain age. In other words, Korean companies often have an internal age limit when recruiting new employees.[7] The reason for such an age limitation is the internal tension that may be created when a person enters the company who is relatively senior in age, but at the same time "junior" to colleagues in terms of job tenure and job title. Such incongruence regarding seniority

Table 9.1 Korean companies' selection process for new employees

Selection stage	Selection contents	Evaluation criteria
(1) Screening of application documents	Review of biographical data, certificates, recommendation letters/references, internship record (for internship trainees)	Age, reputation of high school and university, high school and university major and grades, additional certificates (e.g. English test score, professional certificates), quality of recommendations/references, internship evaluations (when applicable)
(2) Written examinations	Standardized tests of professional or technical knowledge, foreign language proficiency tests, psychological tests	Work related skills and competencies, foreign language proficiencies, aptitude for job
(3) Personal interviews	Interviews with human resource managers and/or managers of job related departments regarding fit between expectations of firm and applicant	Personality, attitude, and motivation towards work and fit with company culture

in terms of different criteria can result in serious conflicts in Korean organizations, as both seniority and hierarchy play vital roles in the Confucian value system and therefore should go hand in hand.

Another crucial evaluation aspect is the personality of an applicant, which is mainly considered at the final stage of the selection process. Even extremely qualified applicants may not be given a job offer unless the interviewers feel that they are strongly motivated for the job and their personality fits well with the company culture. Depending on the company, specific aspects, such as aptness for teamwork, mental openness, or creativity are emphasized.[8]

Regardless of their tough and comprehensive selection criteria when recruiting new employees, Korean companies do not just wait for applicants to send in their documents. They also engage strongly in advertising their job openings. Such advertising activities include the mailing and publication of information materials as well as campus visits at leading universities and company tours for students.[9] In other words, they invest significantly to make sure that highly qualified individuals become aware of their openings and feel attracted to apply. Taken together, Korean companies make extensive efforts to identify, attract, and recruit only the most qualified workers and managers.

Training Tiger employees

Korean companies are very systematic in their efforts to find and recruit the most qualified and motivated employees. As soon as they have hired them, they start training them to maximize their value for the organization. Moreover, this employee training is not a one-time effort for new employees, but basically continues as long as these employees work for the company.

When new employees enter a company, they undergo an intensive orientation program, which typically lasts for one to several months. Often, these programs start even before the official commencement date of employment, being effectively "pre-employment" orientations. The program contents tend to be rather broad and not limited to specific business functions in order to give new employees an overview of the company as a whole. Moreover, they include not only strictly task-related training, but also emphasize team activities, such as mountain climbing, to give new members the opportunity to socialize with their colleagues and to make them familiar with the company's organizational culture.[10] It has been estimated that as much as fifty percent of the overall training time for new employees is dedicated to such socializing and "moral training."[11] Companies also seek specific, innovative ways to accomplish these goals. Hyundai, for example, established a program that paired each new employee before he or she started working for the company with a senior employee to create an informal knowledge transfer channel before official employment.[12]

After finalizing the initial orientation, employees are continuously invited to participate in various training programs. Large companies have developed very extensive and systematic programs that cover modules on all functional business areas and are tailored for different managerial levels, ranging from supervisors to top managers. They also include full scale in-house MBA programs, foreign language courses, and overseas training modules. These trainings reflect the eagerness of Korean companies to educate their employees to become managers with global mindsets who can successfully manage international operations. International activities are given a high priority in the training programs. In 1995, approximately one quarter of the overall training budgets of leading *chaebols* fell to overseas training expenditures.[13]

Companies also give strong incentives to their whole managerial staff to participate in the training programs. Participation in specific programs is often an important factor for being selected for important managerial positions in the future. Therefore, ambitious managers will eagerly participate to build up a strong training and qualification record within their company.

The programs are mostly organized by dedicated training centers, which are run by the company or business group. These corporate training centers were built up from the early stages of Korea's industrialization and subsequently became very widespread. Their number exploded from 16 centers in 1967 to 476 centers in 1976.[14] Nowadays, virtually every medium-sized or large Korean company has one or several training centers for its employees. The companies are making sizeable investments to maintain these centers and create ever more sophisticated programs. They clearly devote a higher proportion of their total financial resources on employee training and development than their counterparts in other industrialized countries. For example, Samsung has been spending 3.5 percent of its payroll for these activities in 1995, compared with 1.5 percent for Motorola.[15] On average, it is estimated that 5 percent of the total working time of employees is set aside for training and development programs.[16]

Overall, it is evident that Korean companies make very systematic training efforts. They invest heavily to develop the skills and capabilities of their employees continuously through participation in highly differentiated programs. The contents of these programs are not purely task related, but also strongly emphasize "moral education" to ensure that the mindsets and attitudes of all employees are in line with the company's values and organizational culture.

Rewarding Tiger employees

Korean companies make strong efforts to recruit very capable and motivated employees and to develop their skills through extensive training. They have also developed elaborate systems to reward them in ways which further spur their motivation to dedicate themselves to their companies and their work.

In Korean firms, all employees are subjected to regular performance evaluations, which take place in a three stage process. First, managers and workers are evaluated by their direct supervisor. Thereafter, this evaluation is reviewed by a senior manager to whom the employee's supervisor reports. Finally, the human resource department collects and standardizes all evaluations.[17] In line with the comprehensive approach Korean companies take towards managing their employees, these evaluations do not only reflect task-related performance, but also social behavior, such as teamwork efforts, initiative, or attitude towards higher ranked managers.[18] As a result of this evaluation, pay increases and promotions are decided. Promotions are a strong incentive for Korean employees to work hard, as they are linked to a person's status, which is highly important in a hierarchical culture driven by Confucian values.

Notwithstanding this elaborated system, evaluations had only a very limited impact on the actual compensation and career paths of many Korean managers and workers until the 1980s. This was for two reasons. First, there was not a strong variation in evaluations between different employees, as managers were reluctant to give them low scores even if they did not perform very well.[19] In the Confucian understanding of paternalistic leadership, many superior managers felt obliged to be lenient with subordinates. Second, pay increases and promotions were often mainly determined by seniority, as measured by the number of years a person had worked for a company. Effectively, employees were moving up the internal ladder according to seniority-linked salary classes and had to wait for a certain number of years until being promoted to the next higher managerial level, almost regardless of their performance.

This system fitted well with the strong emphasis placed on seniority in a Confucian company culture and was very similar to the seniority-based compensation and promotion systems adopted by Japanese companies. Although it often made little difference between employees according to their individual performance, it was still widely accepted during the early stages of Korea's industrialization. This high acceptance again had two reasons. First, real wage and salary levels were rising, thereby allowing everyone to increase their standard of living. Second, many Korean firms could offer a high job security to their workers and managers, as they were growing quickly and therefore normally did not have a reason to remove staff members from their payroll.

Since the 1990s, however, many companies have perceived a strong need to change their compensation and promotion systems, as they have felt they should give stronger incentives for highly performing employees in an increasingly globalized and competitive business environment. One pioneer in changing its human resource management was Doosan Group, which introduced an "annual salary system" that represented a systemic departure from the previous seniority-based salary classes and allowed a stronger differentiation in compensation between high and low performers.[20] Another business group that started introducing stronger performance incentives for its employees in the 1990s was Samsung.

These changes were accelerated during the economic crisis in the years after 1997. Many companies had to lay off workers and managers in large numbers to secure their survival. In other words, the de facto employment security, which Korean firms previously provided for their employees, could no longer be maintained.[21] At the same time, companies were now introducing performance-based incentive systems at a much faster pace than before to enhance their competitiveness.

Table 9.2 shows the employee compensation system that was introduced by Samsung Electronics throughout the late 1990s and the early 2000s. The "basic salary," "performance-based salary," and "holiday support" components largely represent the legacy of the previous, mainly seniority-based compensation system. However, in addition to these components, the company has introduced hefty performance incentives on three levels: the main business unit, the product line organization, and the individual employee. Moreover, it also gives special incentives for core employees in functions regarded as particularly important by the company, such as R&D. In combination, these additional incentives allow the company to differentiate strongly between employees and organizational units according to their contributions to business performance.

Not all Korean companies have changed their compensation systems as radically as Samsung Electronics. However, "annual salary systems" have been broadly introduced since the late 1990s, indicating an overall move towards stronger performance incentives in employee compensation.[22] When compared with established *chaebols*, this tendency is even stronger among venture firms, which do not have a legacy of seniority-based compensation systems and often attract and retain outstanding talent by providing stock options.[23]

At the same time, promotion systems have also become more flexible. Nowadays, more and more young managers are entering the senior managerial and executive ranks of their companies. Samsung, for example, now allows its managers to enter companies' executive ranks in their early forties when they perform strongly.[24] Moreover, individuals from outside are increasingly recruited for high level positions provided they have outstanding skills and capabilities.[25]

Overall, it can be seen that Korean companies have seriously overhauled their compensation and promotion systems throughout the last twenty years to adjust their human resource management to a more competitive environment. Whereas the seniority component in employee compensation still exists, it has become

Table 9.2 Employee compensation system at Samsung Electronics

	Compensation part	Compensation content
Annual salary based on individual contract	Basic salary (60 percent)	Basic compensation to cover living expenses
	Performance-based salary (40 percent)	Additional compensation according to performance by salary class
	Holiday travel support	200 percent of monthly basic salary as travel support for two major holiday seasons (lunar new year and *chuseok*)
	Additional performance-based adjustment	Ranking according to five performance classes Extra compensation of 130 percent of basic salary for highest class Reduction of 15 percent of basic salary for lowest class
Compensation based on separate contract	Incentives for core employees	Separate incentives ranging from 5 million to 150 million KRW annually for highly qualified employees in key functions such as R&D or marketing
Organizational incentives	Productivity incentive	Incentive provided (1) on main business unit and (2) on product line level Performance evaluation according to three ranks Incentive of 150 percent/100 percent/0 percent of basic salary according to evaluation rank on main business unit and product line levels Evaluation based on unit's profit before cost of capital (70 percent) and fulfillment of goals set by CEO (30 percent)
	Profit sharing	Return of 20 percent of total profit on product line level to employees Upper limit: 50 percent of annual salary

Source: Adapted from Choi and Lee, *Managerial values and human resource management at Korea's large business groups,* 143.

much less dominant than it used to be. Interestingly, Korean companies have made these changes at a much faster pace than Japanese companies, which they initially used as models when introducing seniority-based, long-term employment systems.[26] Korean firms now provide strong incentives for capable employees to maximize their contribution to their companies' performance.

At the same time, the factual employment guarantees, which were widespread during the previous decades, have mostly gone since the post 1997 financial crisis. Therefore, employees are aware that they may be laid off if they or the organizational unit they belong to continuously underperform and always need to do their best to keep their jobs. Moreover, many employees are recruited now based on non-permanent contracts with lower salaries and no employment security. After the crisis, the overall proportion of such non-permanent employment has reached about 50 percent in Korea.[27] These employment practices add to the performance pressure on permanently employed managers and workers who often fear that, once laid off, they may not find again such permanent and relatively well paid jobs.

Underlying forces of Korean human resource management

As the discussion of Korean style human resource has shown, the companies place very high demands on their employees. They hire only those applicants who successfully pass a comprehensive selection process and prove to be both highly qualified and strongly motivated to work for their company. They send them to intensive new employee orientations and expect them to participate in further training programs on a regular basis. Furthermore, they increasingly link their compensation and promotion to their performance, thereby exposing them to continuous pressure to show good results. In short, they expect them to be true "Tiger employees" who fully devote themselves to their work and do everything needed to enhance their companies' success.

It is obvious that fulfilling all these expectations requires strong efforts and a high commitment by Korean managers and workers. In fact, they work longer hours than their counterparts in any other OECD country.[28]

Why are Korean workers and managers willing to work so hard and for so long for their companies, much more so than the working populations in other industrialized countries? There are two general features of Korean society which support this outstanding work enthusiasm: a strong hunger for economic success, and an outstanding drive for educational achievement.

A nation hungry for success

Throughout history, the overwhelming majority of Koreans lived in great poverty, and in the country's rigid pre-modern class society there was little chance for most of them to escape from this fate. Most Koreans continuously suffered and struggled for survival.[29]

At the same time, the Korean nation as a whole was also frequently engaged in fights to maintain its independence. Being located between East Asia's two dominant powers, China and Japan, the country was repeatedly exposed to foreign aggression and invasions. With great sacrifices, repeated foreign attempts to take control were fought off over the centuries.[30]

In 1910, however, Korea was annexed by Japan. Subsequently, although the economy was modernized to some extent, and a certain industrial infrastructure was built up under Japanese control as described in Chapter 3, living standards stagnated or even declined. Koreans felt humiliated about being colonized and at the same time continued their fight for survival in their daily lives.[31]

Even after liberation from Japanese rule in 1945, the Korean suffering did not come to an end. The country was divided into two parts controlled by ideologically hostile regimes followed by the Korean War, which destroyed major parts of the country's infrastructure and claimed approximately 3 million lives.[32] As a result, annual per capita income was still below US$100 until the early 1960s,[33] which was lower than that of many other developing countries around the world. The average Korean family was still struggling for sheer survival.

It is useful to review these historical facts to understand the Korean mindset, individually and as a nation, in the subsequent decades after the country's economy started growing at high rates. Having been exposed to so much hardship for such a long time, and being used to fighting for survival, it was only natural for Koreans to do everything they could to change their fate and eventually increase their living standards through hard work. For most of them, it was the first real chance to make a better living. Therefore, there was no question about grabbing this opportunity, even if this meant working for long hours, taking few or no vacations, and sacrificing private life. The devotion of most workers and managers for their work was further amplified by being told by their government and company leaders that their work was part of a national industrialization and development effort.[34] In other words, the hunger for individual economic success was further enhanced by national pride of economic development.

The extraordinary devotion of Koreans to fully dedicate themselves to their work continued over the following decades, even when many of them became quite prosperous. The strong feeling of individual and collective achievement enhanced the willingness to self-sacrifice now in order to secure a better life in the future. So diligent have the Korean employees been that even the Japanese, who stand out for their long working hours and short vacations among industrialized nations, complained that they worked too hard.[35]

A nation driven by education

A second general characteristic of Korean society is a very strong drive for educational achievement. It is clearly related to the country's Confucian tradition, which places high value on education and scholarship. Koreans are very eager to make high investments into their own education as well as that of their children, as high educational achievement brings strong gains in terms of social status and career perspectives.

As long as Korea was a poor economy dominated by agriculture, higher educational aspirations were beyond the means of most people. When the country started industrializing in the 1960s and personal incomes began to increase, however, this situation changed rapidly. Millions of Koreans made great sacrifices to enable their children to go to university or even to study abroad. This trend continued over several decades, resulting in a true education boom.[36]

It also has to be noted that the Korean education system is extremely competitive and selective, particularly at the university entrance level. Entrance examinations at leading universities are extremely difficult to pass, allowing only the very best applicants to enter. Moreover, Korean universities are clearly ranked, and future job prospects are strongly determined by the prestige of the university from which an applicant has graduated. Therefore, Korean middle and high school students are used to studying extremely hard and to being exposed to severe competition.[37]

The results speak for themselves. Almost 100 percent of young Koreans now graduate from high schools and around two thirds of them take a university degree. This makes Korea the number one country in the OECD regarding high school and university graduation rates. Moreover, Korea sends more students to other countries, particularly to the US, than any other OECD country.[38] Whereas, historically, the average education level has been low in Korea because of a lack of economic means, young Koreans are now among the most educated people in the world in their generation, and many of them also have overseas studying experience. Through such global exposure and through education reforms in Korea itself, young Koreans also increasingly acquire critical thinking skills and creativity, qualities which had not been emphasized in previous decades when education was more focused on rote learning. They study hard to become ever more qualified and to differentiate themselves from their peers.

Korean companies can therefore afford to be very selective when recruiting employees, as they can choose from a large pool of competent applicants. Moreover, managers and workers are generally used to continuous learning and studying and tend to view company training programs as an opportunity to further qualify themselves rather than as a burden. Finally, as Koreans are used to strong competitive pressure from their school and college education, introducing competition and performance-based compensation and promotion systems is not overly difficult for companies. In other words, the national education zeal supports all aspects of how human resource management is practiced by Korean companies.

Conclusion

In this chapter, the way Korean firms are recruiting, developing, and rewarding their employees has been discussed. The companies have a very heavy-handed and selective approach when recruiting new employees to make sure that only the most qualified and strongly motivated individuals enter their organization. They train them extensively in order to enable them to make the best possible contribution to their companies' performance. Moreover, over the last two decades, they have a made a transition from seniority-based to performance-based compensation and promotion systems. In short, the companies make comprehensive efforts to turn their managers and workers into true Tiger employees. Comparative research has shown that, in fact, Korean firms are more strongly engaged in such "high-involvement human resource management strategies" than their counterparts from other countries.[39]

It also became clear that Korean style human resource management is supported by two general features of the country's society. First, Koreans work very hard to achieve economic success – for themselves, their company, and their country. Second, they study very hard and make great sacrifices to enable their children to receive the best possible education. Only in the last fifty years have most of them been given an opportunity to work themselves out of poverty and to reach high educational achievements that carry high social status gains in a society with strong Confucian traditions. The endless fight for survival experienced by previous generations has been turned into a fight for wealth and education.

Korean companies have found ideal conditions to implement their specific style of human resource management. They develop their employees, one by one, into highly skilled and capable individuals who are willing to contribute everything in their capacity to their companies' performance. These individual capabilities and attitudes of workers and managers thereby greatly contribute to the success of companies.

Part IV

The present and future of Tiger Management

10 Tiger Management in the world

Meeting the challenge of globalization

> Moving into the 21st century, LG made restless advances to meet the mind of the people of the world. Focusing on electronics, chemicals, communications and services, we went out to make their lives ever more convenient and affluent. From now on, LG will absolutely and until forever leave an image of trust in the hearts of the world's customers.
>
> From LG's 60 year company history[1]

The review of the development of Korean companies in Part II has shown that, within a few decades, Korean companies have transformed themselves from local businesses in a poor and underdeveloped East Asian country to global first tier players that continuously gain market share from their competitors in almost every corner of the world. At least from the 1970s, most of the growth and success of Korean firms has been the result of their international expansion.

The outstanding performance of many Korean companies can be attributed to a peculiar management system, which is named Tiger Management. As discussed in Part III of this volume, Tiger Management is centered on the three core areas of strategy, leadership, and human resource management. Moreover, the specific management style of Korean firms is strongly related to their home country's history, culture, and society.

When being considered together, these two basic observations – the global success of Korean firms and the strong roots of Tiger Management in Korea – bring up the question of how the companies can successfully manage their globalization process. In other words, how and to what extent can Tiger Management be transferred to other countries, and how can Korean companies maintain their organizational efficiency and effectiveness when going global? These are the issues considered in this chapter. After outlining the main aspects of the globalization challenge, it will be analyzed how this challenge is met by the companies. As will be shown, it is again the typical mix of decisive action and flexibility that enables them to manage their globalization process successfully.

Globalization challenges for Korean companies

Generally speaking, when companies are globalizing their business, they face two fundamentally conflicting challenges. On the one hand, they need to be responsive to the local environment in each country and region within which they are operating. On the other hand, they have to maintain a high efficiency level in their worldwide operations. These two goals of local responsiveness and global efficiency are potentially conflicting, as the first one requires customization and the second one calls for standardization.[2] For example, from a local responsiveness viewpoint, it would be ideal to sell customized products in each country in order to match local customer needs and preferences. However, such local product customization potentially hurts global efficiency, as it may prove costly and difficult to develop and produce many different product versions to serve regional preferences. Conversely, from a global efficiency viewpoint, it would be best to sell one standardized product to all customers in the world to minimize development, production, and marketing costs. Such a standardized approach, however, will inevitably have to ignore differences in customer needs across countries. Notwithstanding this conflict between customization and standardization, companies need to find policies in order to be both sufficiently responsive to the environment in each country and globally efficient to compete successfully on a worldwide level.

For Korean companies, the local responsiveness challenge is a particularly great one, as they used to operate only in their East Asian home country, whereas some of the most important markets into which they expanded when going international were in Western countries, which are geographically and culturally distant from a Korean perspective. Moreover, the institutional environment in these industrialized countries is also very different from that in emerging Korea. Not surprisingly, a majority of Korean business executives have cited globalization as the biggest external challenge to their organizations in a recent survey.[3]

The need for localization has, broadly speaking, two main aspects. First, companies need to be responsive to their external business environment. In each country and region, they need to understand the specific needs and requirements of various external stakeholders such as customers, suppliers, government agencies, labor unions, and the media. Second, as soon as the companies establish local operations in other countries, they also need to localize internally. In other words, they need to develop policies in order to manage their international subsidiaries and local workforces in each country effectively.

Meeting the need for global efficiency can be expected to be no less challenging from the viewpoint of Korean companies. They have been used to operating in a geographically rather small country and relying heavily on direct face-to-face communication when managing their workforces and dealing with customers, suppliers, and government officials, as seen in Chapter 8. Therefore, it constitutes a huge task for them to operate a complex network of sites in geographically distant locations.

While being confronted with the need to achieve both local responsiveness and global efficiency, the companies also have to consider how they can transfer Tiger Management to their global operations. As their previous growth and success was clearly the result of their Tiger Management practices, this is an eminently important issue for them. The successful transfer of Tiger Management to other countries and regions may be regarded as a key factor to maintain Korean companies' strong performance in the long term.

How Korean companies deal with globalization

Localization of supplier and customer linkages

As discussed in Chapter 6, Korean firms have aggressively invested, since the 1990s, to create a stronger presence in their major international markets by establishing wholly owned subsidiaries, which often engage in local production. For large *chaebols* such as Samsung or Hyundai, such bold physical localization efforts were facilitated by the existence of major suppliers within the boundaries of their groups.

However, it should be noted that the companies have by no means been dogmatic in their approach to international supplier selection. As case studies from the automobile and electronic industries in China have shown, Korean assemblers did not hesitate to engage with local suppliers if certain supply items were not readily available from group internal sources. In contrast with Japanese companies, which entered lengthy negotiations to persuade suppliers in Japan to follow them abroad, their Korean counterparts readily created stable and reliable local supply chains by working with local suppliers when necessary.[4]

Building such local supplier networks was not always easy. For example, when LG Electronics built assembly operations in Thailand, it found that local suppliers were technologically advanced and held a wide portfolio of leading manufacturers among their customers. Therefore, these suppliers were quite selective in the choice of their business partners, and initially not all of them were eager to work with LG. However, the company eventually succeeded in gaining Thai suppliers through continuous persuasive efforts, which included invitations for executives to visit Korea to show them LG's standing as a global manufacturer. When it proved difficult for some suppliers to deliver their goods on a daily base to the assembly factory on account of a long geographic distance or lack of own transportation equipment, LG purchased delivery trucks and let them constantly circulate between suppliers' plants and its own factory to establish a stable supply chain.[5]

As these examples show, when Korean firms localized their production activities abroad, their clear priority was always to create reliable local supply chains. When vertical integration could be achieved by relying on internal sources, full localization was sought even if this necessitated major investment into wholly owned subsidiaries. When internal supply sources were not available, however, the firms flexibly engaged with local external suppliers. In other words, the highest possible localization of internal and external suppliers has been pursued.

This supply chain localization has proved to be a major asset in customer relations, particularly in emerging markets where local production costs are low, but supply chains tend to be disrupted quite often. In contrast to competitors, Korean firms could deliver their products reliably with stable quality and at low prices in these markets.[6]

However, the companies have made further efforts to win customers and increase their market share in each country and region. One major aspect of these efforts has been the customization of products and customer services according to local needs and preferences.

For example, LG Electronics has become well known for its sales and marketing efforts to satisfy specific customer needs in each country and region. This flexibility has also been extended to product development activities, as the company made strong efforts to customize products according to local customer needs. One famous example has been the development of "Mecca phones" in Muslim countries. These mobile phones include customized features for Muslim users, such as a compass function showing the direction of Mecca and a prayer alarm function. At the same time, LG Electronics entered collaborations with various famous European brands, such as Prada, to strengthen its image among customers.[7] Through the customized development of high end products for the European market, it became recognized as a premium producer in this region.[8]

Similarly, Hyundai Motor has been able to increase its market share in many countries through its intensive localization efforts in product development and marketing. For example, in the US it developed successor models tailored to the preferences of American customers.[9] In India, based on a thorough market survey, it first launched a compact automobile which had the largest local market potential.[10] Moreover, it engaged in intensive customer service and helped local customers with limited financial resources to secure the necessary finance schemes to purchase their cars. It gave customers the feeling that they were not just buying a car, but a relationship. Such relationship oriented marketing efforts proved to be highly effective in an emerging Asian country.[11]

Overall, Korean companies engaged continuously in localizing customer relationships in different countries by intensive product development, marketing, and service efforts to address their specific needs. These efforts can be regarded as a major factor behind the companies' strong performance on their main international markets in recent years. Moreover, their performance was further enhanced by the successful localization of their supply chains, which enabled them to reliably deliver high quality products at low prices.

On a fundamental level, it can also be said that the companies succeeded in transferring important aspects of Tiger Management to other countries in their localization efforts. They boldly invested in local production and marketing and did not shy away from the high risk of such investments. They showed pragmatism and flexibility when engaging with suppliers and customers in each country. Moreover, they also generally managed their localization at a high speed, which often gave them an important advantage over their slower competitors.

Management of international subsidiaries

When establishing new subsidiaries outside their home country, Korean firms initially tend to replicate their domestic organization and management systems. All newly recruited employees are carefully selected and trained. Seniority plays an important role for promotion and compensation, and organizational hierarchies tend to be pronounced. Local executive positions are typically filled with expatriate managers dispatched from Korea.[12]

One particular feature of Korean style management that tends to be particularly widely transferred to international subsidiaries is the holistic approach taken by managers when interacting with and evaluating employees. In other words, human interaction in the workplace is not limited to task-related matters, but also embraces personal and social issues. For example, when Hyundai Motor recruited a large number of employees for its new subsidiary and production site in India, personality, attitude, and motivation were the most important selection criteria.[13] A similarly broad assessment base was set for the ongoing evaluation of managers and workers, as can be seen from Table 10.1.

This integrated approach in dealing with employees often appears to have been received quite well by local workforces, particularly in emerging markets. For example, the management of Hynix's semiconductor factory in China persuaded its local employees to show greater flexibility in working hours than usual, resulting in a productivity exceeding that of its main production site in Korea.[14] Samsung and LG created a Family Ambassador system at their subsidiaries in India where senior executives regularly visited the workers' homes. By showing such caring attitudes, they could minimize potential conflicts with local employees and increase their loyalty.[15]

Table 10.1 Appraisal criteria for executive and non-executive employee groups at Hyundai Motors India

	Executive groups	*Non-executive groups*
Work output	●	●
Quality at work	●	●
Cost consciousness	●	●
Job knowledge	●	●
Interpersonal competence	●	●
Communication	●	●
Attitude	●	●
Creativity	●	
Ability for self-development	●	
Punctuality and attendance		●
Team cooperation		●
Discipline		●

Source: Adapted from Lansbury, Suh, and Kwon, *The Global Korean Motor Industry*, 106.

Although certain features of Tiger Management can be transferred quite effectively to other countries, it cannot be expected that all its aspects will be well received at international subsidiaries around the world, as there are strong cultural differences between Korea and other countries. For instance, workers and managers in egalitarian Western countries may find the hierarchical organization or the strong consideration for seniority in the Korean management system hard to accept. In some countries, local employees may not be willing to work as hard as their counterparts in Korea, as the local culture attributes a higher value to leisure activities. The strong Korean emphasis on teamwork may also not be well received in countries with more individualistic cultures.[16]

Notably, however, Korean companies have regularly shown a high flexibility in adjusting their approaches when they became aware that the transfer of their domestic management system resulted in conflicts with local employees. For example, when a manager was dispatched by his company to Mexico to direct the companies' local production facility, he noticed that workers were unhappy as they felt that their views and opinions were not sufficiently considered by Korean expatriates. The Korean CEO could, however, gradually change the atmosphere and gain the trust of employees by regularly meeting with and listening to Mexican supervisors who became mediators between workers and executives.[17] Hyundai Motor created a works committee in its Indian subsidiary that convened regularly to identify and resolve conflicts between Korean executives and local workers. Hyundai subsequently revised its practices to promote greater loyalty among its employees.[18] It also added some hierarchical ranks in its organization to give a higher social status to certain groups of workers who were unhappy with the initial organizational setup.[19] The Managing Director of LG Electronics in India made comprehensive efforts to understand the local culture and employees' opinions and adjusted managerial policies accordingly. As a result, LG Electronics became very successful in the Indian market thanks to its strong localization.[20]

Korean companies have also engaged in elevating the foreign language proficiency and cross-cultural competence of their expatriate managers. They are investing heavily into new training programs for managers who are to be dispatched to foreign subsidiaries in the future. These programs are offered at various managerial levels and diverse in contents, ranging from developing experts for specific countries or regions, to competence building regarding the management of local workforces in international operations, to MBA programs designed to elevate the general understanding of the global business environment. At Samsung alone, more than 3,000 managers have participated in these programs since the 1990s.[21]

At the same time, the pre-acquired level of international experience and, therefore, of language proficiency and cross-cultural competence, is rapidly increasing among Korean managers.[22] While the overseas living experience was quite exceptional among Koreans until a few decades ago, it has now almost become the norm in the educated young generation to move for a while to a foreign country for school or university education. As discussed in Chapter 9, the general education drive is extremely strong in Korea, and as a part of this tendency, young Koreans and their parents make extraordinary efforts to achieve entrance into prestigious overseas high schools and universities, particularly in English-speaking countries.

As a result, the competence of expatriate managers in speaking English and local languages and in dealing with non-Korean workforces has rapidly advanced in recent years. This trend can be expected to continue in the future when the current young generation of managers works its way up to the more senior levels of corporate hierarchies.

Additionally, the companies also make intense efforts to recruit outstanding local talent for managerial positions at their international subsidiaries. These non-Korean managers are extensively trained and sent to Korea in increasing numbers for specific training programs in order to give them a full understanding of their companies' culture, organization, and management systems. Thereafter, they return to their home countries and assume managerial positions at local subsidiaries.[23] In the same vein, there is a broad tendency among Korean companies to reduce the number of expatriate managers and replace them with local managers who assume more and more responsibility. In fact, this localization of management appears to have elevated the international subsidiary performance of many Korean companies, with LG Electronics being a well known example.[24] Overall, although it cannot be denied that expatriates still play quite a dominant role in the management of international subsidiaries, some leading Korean firms have become serious about educating local managers and giving more responsibility to them.

Some companies have even gone one step further in recent years regarding the roles they give to their international subsidiaries. They transfer knowledge from these subsidiaries back to Korea. Samsung Electronics, for example, is systematically seeking input from its global design centers when developing its next generation products in Korea.[25] Such willingness to learn from foreign subsidiaries shows the companies' mental openness, as they do not insist that international subsidiaries always have to follow their domestic management systems, but that headquarters in return may also learn from them. It may be regarded as a natural behavior for Korean companies, which had absorbed a lot of foreign knowledge when catching up with global competitors during previous decades.

Taken together, while most Korean companies initially follow the model of their domestic operations when designing the organizational structures and management systems of newly established foreign subsidiaries, they show a high flexibility and adaptiveness thereafter in order to resolve conflicts with local employees and to increase their commitment and motivation. According to a long-term country manager, the basic assumption when managing overseas subsidiaries is that everything there should work according to the local standard, not the Korean standard.[26]

Korean expatriate managers become more and more competent in foreign languages and cross-cultural communication. Moreover, the companies over time increasingly rely on local managers in the management of foreign subsidiaries and give them more responsibility while extensively training them to make them familiar with their management systems and corporate cultures. In other words, while often running into problems in the early stages after establishing foreign subsidiaries, attributable to a lack of understanding of the local culture, the companies become more and more proficient in the internal localization of their global operations. They localize and at the same time retain crucial components of Tiger Management, namely, flexibility, determination, and creating a strong motivation and high commitment among their managers and workers.

Global coordination and control

Companies need to coordinate and control their global operations on several levels. First, they need to decide the overall configuration of their worldwide activities – in other words, to determine which activities are conducted where. Second, they need to develop appropriate organizational structures for these activities. Specifically, they have to create organizational units and to divide competencies, responsibilities, and reporting lines among them. Third, they need to apply efficient and effective organizational processes to manage all their global activities on an ongoing basis.

As discussed in Chapter 6, Korean firms generally tend to replicate their integrated domestic operations by building large manufacturing complexes in foreign countries. This approach is not limited to the very largest business groups, but can be also found among other *chaebols*. Lotte Group, for example, is currently building multiple "Lotte Towns" in emerging markets and aiming to integrate its various business interests which include hotels, department stores, supermarkets, restaurants, confectionary production, and home shopping as much as possible at each location.[27] The groups are replicating their integrated operations globally to maximize vertical and horizontal synergies. At the same time, they seek to transfer the organizational dynamism that augmented their growth in Korea to other countries and regions.

Regarding the detailed design of overseas operations, however, the companies are flexible. They do not insist on replicating all organizational arrangements from Korea in other countries. Hyundai Motor, for example, has designed its overseas production hubs in various ways in response to the local environment. It chose a factory design with relatively little automation and labor-intensive production technology in countries with low labor cost such as Turkey and India, but applied state-of-the-art technology in its production site in the technologically advanced US.[28] A similar pragmatism has been observed for Hyundai suppliers when they followed their customer and built production sites outside Korea.[29]

On the level of organizational design, Korean companies initially used to centralize most control at their headquarters. Managers in each foreign subsidiary had to report directly to the global headquarters in Korea and needed their approval for all important business matters.

Over time, however, some companies have given more autonomy to international subsidiaries. According to a senior Korean expatriate, global headquarters now provide only general guidelines and set business targets, giving subsidiary managers a free hand in day-to-day operations on how to achieve these targets.[30] Organizational structures have also been changed accordingly. Specifically, the establishment of "regional headquarters" has become popular.[31] Such regional headquarters oversee the business for one important region and control each subsidiary within this region. Thereby, the Korean headquarters are giving up direct control over international subsidiaries, and the business environment in each region can be considered to develop customized strategies.

Some companies have been going back and forth to find the best global organizational structure for their business. Samsung Electronics introduced a system of eight regional headquarters around the world in 1996 to decentralize its organization and create more regional synergies. However, the company soon realized that the benefits of localization were much smaller than expected. At the time, all executive positions at regional headquarters were still occupied with Korean managers who did not all have a sufficient understanding of the need for regional differentiation and tended to replicate their domestic Korean business and management in their regions. In other words, the company's organizational structure was running ahead of its organizational culture and the mindset of its managers in terms of localization. Therefore, the company reorganized again in 1998 and introduced a global product manager organization, which was located at the Korean headquarters but allowed for different approaches according to the type of product being dealt with. In 2001, another reorganization to a global business manager system followed to widen the perspective of division managers.[32]

Overall, a gradual decentralization of control can be observed in the global operations of Korean companies. It has to be conceded that, compared with Western companies, their organizational structures are still regarded as highly centralized. This is also reflecting the genuinely centralized and hierarchical structure of Korean companies. However, similar to other managerial aspects, the companies are willing to change their structure in response to business needs and thereby prove to be pragmatic in their policies.

The ongoing management and coordination of Korean companies' global operations is largely conducted by expatriate managers who control each subsidiary. As expatriate managers can be an effective means of international knowledge transfer, this arrangement appears to be appropriate for Korean firms that place high importance on the comprehensive transfer of their management systems and corporate cultures to foreign operations.[33] Additionally, headquarter executives tend to make frequent visits to international subsidiaries to interact directly with their managerial staff.[34] Although the companies also use IT technologies extensively for their global management, this emphasis on personal communication appears to be well aligned with the strong leadership by senior managers, which is an integral part of Tiger Management.

Conclusion

In this chapter, it has been shown how Korean companies are coping with the globalization challenge. Specifically, their efforts to make their worldwide operations locally responsive and globally efficient and the extent to which they could transfer Tiger Management to their subsidiaries in other countries have been reviewed.

When setting up international production subsidiaries, Korean firms prefer to establish vertically integrated supply chains with internal suppliers. However, when such internal supply sources are not available, they readily engage with local suppliers and flexibly adjust to their needs. Moreover, Korean companies have often customized their products and marketing efforts in each country according to local preferences, more so than their global competitors from Western countries or Japan. This has often given them a strong competitive advantage, particularly in emerging markets.

In contrast, the internal localization of international subsidiaries appears not to have been very high at the initial stage of operations, as most companies tended to replicate their organization and management systems from Korea. However, when facing acceptance problems with local employees, the companies tend to adjust their approaches flexibly in response to the needs of their workforces in each country to make sure that local managers and workers remain motivated to work for them. The insufficient knowledge of the local languages and business cultures by Korean executives who were sent as expatriate managers to run international subsidiaries often appears to have been a key problem for internal localization. However, this problem has been diminished in recent years, as the companies conduct extensive training programs to prepare their managers for international assignments, and as Koreans in general become more globalized in their mindsets from extensive living experiences in other countries. While Korean firms may still be lagging behind leading Western firms regarding the inter-cultural competence and language proficiency of their expatriates, they have made substantial advances regarding these aspects in recent years.

Finally, Korean companies also place high value on integrating their international operations properly and thereby achieve a high global efficiency. The replication of their domestic organizational structures in other countries helps them with meeting these objectives, as similar organizations are easier to integrate and control than dissimilar ones. Moreover, they rely to a high extent on the leadership of expatriate managers and of headquarter executives who make frequent visits to international subsidiaries to instill their organizational cultures in foreign operations.

Taken together, we can see that Korean companies make strong endeavors to meet the challenge of globalization. Not all their international operations are successful from the outset as they experience huge differences between the business cultures in Korea and in other countries, both externally and internally. However, they remain determined to succeed and react swiftly and decisively to the challenges and problems they are facing in each country and region. In this sense, while having to adjust various managerial policies to meet local demands and preferences, they largely succeed not only in globalizing, but also in transferring the core components of Tiger Management to other countries. At the forefront are bold investments, a strong determination to succeed, swift, flexible and decisive responses to challenges, and creation of strong organizational cultures and a high commitment and motivation of employees through the leadership of senior managers. As a result, they frequently beat their local and global competitors in many countries and regions around the world.

11 Dynamic Korea

Domestic challenges for Tiger Management

> The linchpin of management in the information era consists of the proper under-
> standing of social change. The role of senior executives is to transform the com-
> pany and organization in line with the overwhelming requirements of the market
> economy and social currents. Only those companies that lead such transformations
> can have a chance of success.
>
> Lee Woohee, former CEO, Samsung S1 Corporation[1]

Tiger Management is not only challenged by globalization, as discussed in the previous chapter, but also from within Korea itself. The country's economy and society change so quickly that the buzzword of "Dynamic Korea" is, in fact, very much in line with reality.

The profound changes in Korea can be observed from various angles. The Korean economy has been shaken by two major crises: the Asian financial crisis in the late 1990s and the deep global recession in 2008/09 after the default of Lehman Brothers, a leading US investment bank. At the same time, business-government relations have changed drastically in Korea during the last two decades. Although the government strongly supported companies until the 1980s, as a part of its industrialization policy, it became much more critical regarding the governance structures of *chaebols* and their strong influence on the economy from the 1990s. The country's society has witnessed the rise of the labor movement following democratization in the late 1980s and, more recently, the ascendency of women in the corporate world. Lastly, the value systems of Koreans have also been undergoing profound changes in recent years. Employees are less willing than in the past to sacrifice themselves for their companies and to follow the directions of corporate leaders unconditionally. All these developments are, in different ways, exerting pressure on Korean companies to adjust their management systems to a rapidly changing environment.

The shifts in Korea's society, economy, and culture, and the ways in which they constitute challenges for Tiger Management, will be reviewed below in detail.

Thereafter, the companies' policies to accommodate to these changes will be analyzed. As will be shown, Korean companies stand up to these domestic challenges in a similar way to how they are dealing with globalization. They adjust swiftly when necessary, but at the same time keenly preserve the essence of Tiger Management: entrepreneurial ambition, speed, flexibility, strong leadership, and highly motivated human resources.

Domestic challenges for Korean companies

Economic crises and changes in business-government relations

The Korean economy has been exposed to two major crises since its OECD ascendency in 1996, which symbolized its global recognition as an industrialized country. The upheaval in the years after 1997 was fundamentally threatening to the country as a whole, as discussed in Chapter 5. It also forced many companies into bankruptcy or restructuring. More recently, Korea was shaken again by the shockwaves of the global recession after the default of Lehman Brothers in 2008. Although this crisis was not as devastating by far as the previous one, from a Korean perspective, it nonetheless posed major threats for a country deeply integrated into the world economy when global supply chains suddenly collapsed.[2]

The two crises had a deep impact on the relationship between the Korean government and the *chaebols*. In short, they resulted in strong pressure that the government, responding to international obligations and public opinion, exerted on the business groups to change various aspects of their management systems.

As discussed in Chapters 3 and 4, the government actively supported business groups between the 1960s and the 1980s to develop and grow. Following the transition to democracy in 1987 and the election of a civilian president, Kim Young-sam, in 1992, this direct support faded. However, as the government focused on financial deregulation in this period and no longer attempted to interfere directly with business decisions, *chaebols* could continue their expansion strategies largely undisturbed.[3]

This situation changed drastically in the years after 1997. As reviewed in detail in Chapter 5, when the government of President Kim Dae-jung implemented its bailout deal with the IMF, it exerted strong pressure on business groups to reorganize, reduce their debt, and improve their corporate governance. For the first time in decades, the *chaebols* had to deal with a government that was not only interfering, but also, from their perspective, quite unfriendly. The government pressure on *chaebols* continued during the government of President Roh Moo-hyun in the years after 2002.[4]

The impact of the economic crisis of 2008/2009 on Korea was not as dramatic and long lasting as that of the post 1997 financial crisis. Nonetheless, public

At the same time, the Korean government has engaged in gender equality legislation since the 1980s to fight discrimination of women in the workplace. In 1987, the Equal Employment Act formally gave women equal labor rights. Subsequently, the law was revised several times to establish greater legal control over discriminative practices in recruitment, training, allocation, and promotion. A Ministry of Gender Equality was created in 2001 to institutionalize the legal and administrative surveillance of corporate practices. In 2006, the Equal Employment Act introduced an affirmative action policy. It requires companies with 1,000 or more employees to report on their gender specific employment by type of work and by rank.[14] Finally, women are now also protected by a Maternity Protection Law against pressure to resign from their jobs when they become pregnant.[15] They are entitled to up to three months of employer or insurance paid maternity leave.[16]

These legal regulations, and the underlying shifts in Korean society that induced them, are challenging corporate cultures which used to rely heavily on informal communication and bonding through after work social gatherings. In many companies, these gatherings may at times be accompanied by heavy alcohol consumption or even end up in bars where employees are entertained by female hostesses.[17] Such customs are apparently not designed to accommodate female employees, thereby often excluding them from practically important informal communication or even alienating them to the point that they resign from their jobs. Aside from gender related equal opportunity legislation, Korean companies can ill afford to waste female talent in an age when fully utilizing the potential of highly skilled and talented employees becomes a crucial factor in global competition.

Changes in value systems

A third dimension of the domestic challenge for Tiger Management is rooted in changes in Korean workers' and managers' value systems. As discussed earlier, the loyalty of employees to their companies has been greatly supported by Confucian values, which emphasize hard work, group harmony, and obedience to senior people.

Whereas these Confucian values have by no means disappeared from Korean culture and society, other values have gained in relative importance over the last decades. As a result of the country's rapid modernization, opening, and globalization, younger people tend to behave more individualistically than their parents and grandparents. They have not experienced the economic hardships of previous generations and give less priority to material goals, such as monetary income, when compared with intangible elements such as quality leisure time with their families or work satisfaction. In a recent survey, Koreans with a college degree or more ranked "income" only fourth among their job selection criteria behind "stability," "suitability," and "promotion opportunities."[18]

This tendency to pursue personal agendas and priorities more actively has been further triggered by the IT revolution in Korea. While Koreans always cultivated their personal social networks based on school ties or regional ties, meetings with friends and acquaintances used to take place predominantly in face-to-face settings and were therefore quite limited in number and frequency because of time restrictions given their long working hours. This changed after Korea became one of the world's leading countries in Internet broadband connectivity and telecommunication network density since the turn of the millennium. Most Koreans, particularly in the younger age groups, always carry their portable digital devices and communicate with their friends on a daily base using multiple communication channels and social networks.[19] The resulting increase in personal communication density has not only increased transparency across organizations, but also reduced the relative weight of companies as social anchors in the perceptions of their employees. In other words, interaction with company colleagues dominates the social lives of Korean employees less than before.

Younger Koreans also have different views about leadership and group harmony from previous generations. Students have been found to regard conflict as "acceptable if it results in constructive change" and leadership as "to be challenged and replaced if necessary."[20] Similar trends can also be observed for company employees. According to a senior manager, lower ranked managers and workers tend to regard their superiors as "leaders rather than bosses" and expect "guidance rather than orders" from them.[21] Thus, whereas Korean company employees still have a strong perception that their superiors should give them guidance and direction, they do not follow them as unconditionally as they used to.

In sum, changes in the value systems of Koreans are also challenging some traditional aspects of Tiger Management, such as top-down decision making or the expectation that employees sacrifice their private lives and unconditionally devote themselves to their work and their companies. Younger Koreans, while not abandoning Confucian values altogether, are becoming more individualistic and less receptive to authoritarian leadership.

Companies' responses

Corporate governance reforms

The various laws and regulations introduced by the Korean government during the Asian financial crisis, and their influence on corporate governance, have been reviewed in Chapter 5. In short, business groups reduced their financial debts, disposed of non-essential assets, and introduced outside directors onto their boards and greater transparency in their financial reports.

After the crisis, the corporate governance of Korean firms has further gradually improved. For example, the proportion of external directors on corporate boards increased from 24.8 percent in 1999 to 36.4 percent in 2006. Among the largest firms with assets of more than two trillion KRW, the ratio of external directors reached 58.2 percent in the same year.[22]

However, the general perception is that owner families still keep a firm control over business groups, and the methods used to retain this control are often not particularly helpful for establishing transparent corporate governance. Among the largest *chaebols*, only the LG and the GS groups have created official holding companies for their group internal control.[23] Most groups still use complicated circular shareholding structures to allow owner families to exert more control than would normally be possible with their shareholding capital. The transition of ownership control to the next generation is also often accompanied by transactions which appear to be designed to minimize tax payments and which are regarded by some observers as violations of other shareholders' rights. For example, Samsung Chairman Lee Kun-hee helped his son Lee Jae-yong to assume control of Samsung Everland, the factual holding company of the group, by allowing him to purchase corporate bonds at a low price.[24]

Another sensitive area is the strategic planning and control of business groups that has been conducted by chairmen's planning offices, as discussed in Chapter 8. Since the financial crisis, these offices are no longer allowed as independent, private organizations.[25] Therefore, they have been moved either to holding companies or to other key group companies, but effectively kept intact as planning organizations on a smaller scale.[26]

However, there are also important governance aspects where *chaebols'* reform efforts went beyond formal legal compliance and made essential changes in their management systems. One such aspect is the transfer of managerial power from group owners to professional managers. For example, the outstanding performance of Samsung Electronics during the last fifteen years is widely perceived to be primarily the achievement of Yun Jong-yong, who was the company's CEO between 1996 and 2008. Samsung Chairman Lee Kun-hee mostly delegated the management of the huge company to him.[27] Similar power transfers have occurred in many *chaebols* over the last two decades. Chairmen and owner families still typically reserve the right to make or approve major strategic decisions, but many of them have gradually retreated from the everyday business of their groups.

Companies have also embraced transparency as one of their major corporate values. This tendency is exemplified by the slogan of "*jeongdo kyeongyeong*" which may be roughly translated as "integrity management" and which essentially represents transparency and corporate social responsibility. "*Jeongdo kyeongyeong*" is recently emphasized by LG[28] and Samsung,[29] among others.

Development of supplier relations

Throughout the previous decades, large Korean firms often focused to a high extent on keeping an upper hand when dealing with their suppliers, and on continuous cost cutting through price reductions for supply items. Therefore, suppliers often felt squeezed out by their customer firms, which allegedly did not allow them to accumulate sufficient resources to grow technologically stronger. As most SMEs in the Korean manufacturing sector are suppliers for large assembling firms,[30] the relationships between customers and supplier firms are typically framed in Korea as those between large companies and SMEs.

The large firms' attitudes appear to have gradually changed since the turn of the millennium, however. Compared with simple cost reduction, they focus more and more on the quality and technological content of their supply items. As a consequence, they increasingly assist their suppliers with solving technical and managerial problems and let them participate in the development of business plans.

This shift in supplier relations has already created some clear results. For example, over the last decade the rapid growth of Hyundai Motor was accompanied by a similar growth of its suppliers.[31] In a recent survey of suppliers in the automobile, machinery, chemical, and electronic industries, a majority of respondents indicated that they were treated quite fairly by their main customers. Moreover, most of them gave medium or high assessments regarding the extent they could influence the customer firms' business planning and the amount of technical and managerial assistance they received.[32]

Recently, many large business groups and firms, such as Samsung, LG, SK, POSCO, KT, and STX have supported the governmental campaign for "co-prosperity" and pledged to support their suppliers more actively and share their profits fairly.[33] Overall, whereas the dominant position of large final product assemblers in the Korean manufacturing sector is still undeniable, there is a clear shift in supplier relations towards a stronger focus on product quality and technological capabilities. In other words, many large firms are seeking a more balanced relationship with their suppliers.

Changes in industrial relations and human resource management policies

A major turning point in Korea's industrial relations after the country's democratization was the Asian financial crisis. A tripartite commission with representatives from companies, labor unions, and the government was set up to discuss ways on how to deal with the crisis situation. The dismissal of workers was made easier for companies through an amendment of the Labor Standards Act. In return, workers' rights were strengthened, and, in the 2000s, the five day working week was gradually introduced.[34] In short, a somewhat more collaborative relationship between companies and labor unions could be established, though hostilities continued to occur at some companies. As labor unions in Korea are mainly organized on the company level,[35] there is a strong variation in the quality of industrial relations between specific companies and business groups.

In the most recent global recession after the collapse of Lehman Brothers, the collaboration between companies and labor unions reached a new quality. Within a few months after the outbreak of the crisis, both sides reached a comprehensive agreement joined by the government. Labor unions agreed to wage freezes or reductions when necessary, and companies promised to avoid layoffs whenever possible. Consequently, large-scale dismissals of workers could be avoided this time, as company vacations were greatly extended, often on an unpaid basis.[36]

Overall, industrial relations have become much more peaceful in Korea over the last two decades, as most labor unions have become more realistic in their demands and companies' executives are more willing to negotiate with union representatives on an even stance. As a result, the number of labor disputes and accompanying economic losses has gradually decreased and is now approaching the average of OECD countries.[37]

As seen in Chapter 9, Korean companies have also made significant changes in their human resource management since the 1990s, which accelerated during and after the Asian financial crisis. They focus more on performance-based incentives and less on seniority when rewarding and promoting their employees. This shift shows the companies' intentions to motivate their employees to work hard and perform strongly, but also reflects the ongoing value changes among Koreans towards stronger individualism.

The companies have continued to update their human resource management in recent years to stay in tune with the changing values of their employees. When recruiting new staff members, for example, large groups such as Samsung and LG have introduced new test methods, which are focused on applicants' capabilities and personality rather than their education history.[38] They also conduct "blind interviews" where the universities from which applicants have graduated are not revealed to interviewers.[39] The intention of this policy is remove institutional bias from the selection process and make sure that applicants are solely evaluated based on their individual capabilities. Corporate training programs have shifted towards stronger specialization, as companies need more and more specialists to succeed in competition.[40] This stronger focus on specialized skill formation also reflects a general trend towards more specific, individualized interests among employees.

One major trend among Korean companies is to increase the vacation days of their employees and to reduce their working hours. Annual vacations, which typically used to be just a few days, have been extended to around two weeks.[41] More importantly, the number of total working hours has been rapidly reduced in recent years. As can be seen from Figure 11.1, the average number of hours Koreans work in one year has decreased from 2,677 in 1990 to 2,193 in 2010. This represents a reduction of approximately eighteen percent, and most of this reduction has taken place over the last ten years. Whereas Korean employees still work for much longer than their counterparts in most other developed countries, it is clear that companies have given them more time for their personal lives.

Aside from this overall trend towards lightening the work burden of employees, companies have made their working rules more flexible, particularly for white-collar workers. A recently popular scheme is "smart work," essentially allowing employees to work from anywhere outside their offices while being connected with others through IT devices.[42] Companies have also streamlined their organizations by reducing the number of hierarchical layers and introducing team-based work systems.[43] Such organizational reforms have been made to reduce internal bureaucracy, but should also have raised the motivation of younger employees who prefer to work in a less hierarchical organization.

Finally, companies have also started to recruit female employees for managerial career paths more actively. The female ratio among all managers in Korea has increased from 2.2 percent in 1993 to 6.7 percent in 2000 to 10.7 percent in 2008.[44] Whereas this ratio is still very low when compared with other OECD countries, where it is typically at 20–30 percent,[45] the increasing number of women

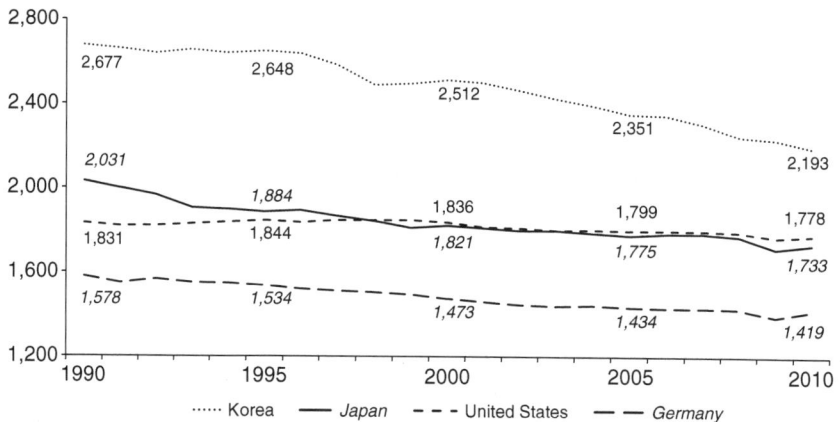

Figure 11.1 Annual working hours in Korea and other selected OECD countries.

Source: OECD, *OECD Statistical Extracts: Average annual hours actually worked per worker.*

managers shows that the companies are becoming aware of the need to make more use of female talent. In fact, case studies of women managers show that their strong skills in leadership, communication, and customer orientation have greatly elevated the performance of their companies.[46]

Changes in leadership style

Although changes in the leadership style of managers are hard to measure in quantitative terms, there is no doubt that many Korean managers are adjusting their approaches. According to a senior manager, subordinates need to be induced to follow directions through persuasion, as they will not be highly committed if simply being given orders.[47] At a different company, senior line managers are induced by executive directors to exert leadership by showing strong professional competencies and creating business plans by themselves instead of relying on their subordinates.[48] Overall, the leadership style of Korean managers appears to be shifting towards a stronger emphasis on persuasion through professional competency.

Such changes in communication methods do not mean, however, that leadership in Korean companies is becoming strongly participative. According to a middle manager, "it is not possible to argue with bosses, as they are almighty." Another one perceives the "strict hierarchies" in companies as still being intact.[49] Subordinated employees in Korean companies still appear to be expected to follow and execute directions without engaging in lengthy discussions.

Taken together, the leadership style of Korean managers appears to have become softer and less authoritarian to accommodate to the attitudes of young co-workers who expect to be instructed professionally and persuasively about managerial policies. However, internal hierarchies as such are still firmly in place, and employees are expected to implement managerial directions swiftly.

Conclusion

In this chapter, the multiple challenges Tiger Management is facing from inside Korea have been analyzed. The country's economy and society, as well as the value systems of individual Koreans, are rapidly changing. These changes force companies to adjust their management systems in many ways, to address the needs of their employees as well as of external stakeholders.

Since the Asian financial crisis, business groups have been under strong pressure to improve their corporate governance. New laws and regulations forced them, for example, to submit consolidated annual financial reports on the group level and to accept outside directors onto their boards. Whereas the groups comply with these requirements, most of them are still kept under the firm control of their owner families. However, many *chaebol* chairmen have also delegated more power to professional managers.

Most companies have made significant improvements in their relations with labor unions and suppliers. Although there are still more labor disputes in Korea than in most other OECD countries, industrial relations are much more peaceful and productive now than they were two decades ago. Many final assemblers have also elevated the quality of their supplier relations by emphasizing product quality over cost reductions, helping their suppliers to increase their technological capabilities, and involving them more actively in their business planning.

Furthermore, the transition of human resource management towards more individual incentives, which started in the 1990s, has continued in many companies. Working hours have been significantly reduced, and working rules become more flexible. Corporate hierarchies have been flattened. Companies are also beginning to recruit women more actively for managerial positions. The leadership style of managers is becoming less authoritarian and more communicative, though not necessarily participative.

There are apparently some aspects in which Korean companies should further strengthen their efforts. A lot of excellent female talent is still hired by foreign companies' Korean subsidiaries, as male applicants are favored in the recruiting process of local companies, or female applicants regard foreign companies as more attractive because of their more open and globalized corporate cultures.[50] Alternatively, many Korean women also open their own businesses. In 2003, there were around 1.1 million women-owned businesses in Korea, equivalent to 37.2 percent of all companies. This ratio is expected to surpass fifty percent in the near future.[51] Furthermore, many young employees are leaving large *chaebol* companies, as they regard the working hours as too long or the company clture as too strict.[52] This illustrates the companies' difficulties in accommodating the rapid changes in Korean society into their management systems and organizations.

Overall, however, it can be clearly said that most companies managed to adjust reasonably well to the rapid changes in Korea. They have become more modern, open, and flexible and at the same time retained the key elements of Tiger Management: aggressive business planning, quick decision making, fast implementation, strong leadership, and strong motivation of employees. In other words, Tiger Management has stood up not only to the challenge of globalization, as seen in the previous chapter, but also to the challenge of domestic change in Korea.

12 Studying Tiger Management
Lessons for non-Korean companies

> The operative assumption today is that someone, somewhere, has a better idea; and the operative compulsion is to find out who has that better idea, learn it, and put it into action – fast.
>
> Jack Welch, former CEO of General Electric[1]

Throughout this book, it has been shown that Korean companies have been extraordinarily successful throughout the last fifty years, and that their success can be attributed to their specific management style. Moreover, it has also been made clear that Tiger Management has not only worked in one country or in one specific historical situation. In fact, many Korean firms have successfully implemented Tiger Management at their overseas subsidiaries, as seen in Chapter 10. Additionally, Tiger Management has been adjusted quite effectively to the rapidly changing business environment in Korea throughout the last decades, as shown in Chapter 11.

Given the remarkable effectiveness of Tiger Management and its proven transferability across various business environments, it appears to be high time that non-Korean companies started considering in earnest what they can learn from their Korean counterparts. Therefore, the transferability of Tiger Management from a non-Korean perspective will be the focus of this last chapter.

First, the issue of international transfer of management practices and potential obstacles to such transfer will be discussed in general. Then potential hurdles and limitations for adopting Tiger Management in particular will be identified. Based on these considerations, this book will be concluded by a summary of the essence of Tiger Management and by some suggestions for non-Korean companies on how they may adopt it. Overall, it appears that many of its important aspects can be transferred across cultures and regions if non-Korean companies study it seriously and muster the patience that is needed for a successful adoption of managerial practices.

Can Tiger management be adopted?

Transferring management knowledge across borders

Business history is full of cases of international transfer of management practices. In fact, most multinational enterprises regard continuous knowledge transfer between headquarters and international subsidiaries as essential for becoming and staying competitive. However, such adoption of best practices often also takes place across the organizational boundaries of companies. In the field of operations and supply chain management, for example, automated line production, initially introduced by Ford, quickly spread around the world in the first half of the twentieth century and helped to achieve dramatic advances in efficiency and cost reduction. In the last two decades, the concept of lean production, first developed by Toyota, was intensively studied and introduced by many non-Japanese companies and helped them to regain competitiveness.[2] More generally, as global benchmarking has become a standard practice in many industries, companies around the world eagerly observe their rivals and try to understand and adopt the best practices of successful competitors whenever possible.

Studies of the international transfer of management practices have shown, however, that there are often substantial hurdles for their successful adoption. For example, when General Motors (GM) set up a joint manufacturing plant with Toyota to study and absorb its lean production system, little knowledge transfer to GM's other sites was achieved in the first years of the joint factory's operation. It took the company considerable time to establish effective means and channels of transferring and absorbing the managerial knowledge.[3]

Generally speaking, several factors influence the effectiveness of the international transfer of managerial knowledge.[4] The receiving side needs to have a sufficient motivation and learning capacity to absorb the knowledge. It is also important that the knowledge source is willing and motivated to share the relevant information. Moreover, knowledge transmission channels between the giving and the receiving sides need to be established and should be as broad and diverse as possible.

Another dimension that complicates the international transfer of managerial knowledge is the cultural distance between the knowledge source and the receiving unit. The larger this cultural distance, the more difficult and costlier the knowledge transfer tends to be.[5] Managers and organizations have bigger difficulties understanding the value of managerial practices when they originate from a culturally very different location. To illustrate, it took managers in Western countries much longer to fully understand and appreciate the value of Japanese style lean management than their counterparts in more nearby countries such as Korea, thereby delaying their efforts to absorb the related knowledge. The potential for misunderstandings in the transfer process is also much higher when the two sides are culturally very dissimilar.

In sum, although the international transfer of effective management practices have become common not only within, but also between companies, strong efforts and patience are needed for an effective knowledge transfer. Moreover, cultural differences between the sharing and the receiving side also need to be considered when initiating such international transfer processes.

Transferring Tiger Management

As the contents of this book have revealed, Tiger Management has given Korean companies strong competitiveness in a wide range of industries. They have repeatedly won competitive battles with Western as well as with Japanese rivals and continuously gained global market share. Therefore, studying and adopting Tiger Management should be basically attractive for companies around the globe, regardless of their country of origin.

As with international knowledge transfer in general, however, cultural distance is also relevant for the transfer of Tiger Management to other countries. From this viewpoint, it can be expected that Korean management practices are easier to absorb for companies in nearby Asian countries, which are culturally similar to Korea, than for their counterparts in Western countries. It is therefore not surprising that the management system of leading Korean companies, such as Samsung Electronics, has raised particular interest in countries such as China[6] or Japan[7].

This does not mean, however, that Tiger Management cannot be transferred to culturally and geographically distant regions, for example Europe or the Americas. The fact that Korean companies have successfully localized their operations in most regions around the globe, as discussed in Chapter 10, proves the opposite. It may just need more preparation and effort to adopt Tiger Management in these regions when compared with East Asian countries.

Aside from the general issue of cultural distance, there are some specific issues related to Korean firms that may give the impression that Tiger Management is applicable only to certain types of companies. One such aspect is the predominance of *chaebols* in the discourse about the management and performance of Korean companies. It cannot be denied that large groups such as Samsung, LG, Hyundai Motor, and SK play a leading role in Korean business at home and abroad. This does not mean, however, that Tiger Management is only practiced by or relevant for such large business groups. As shown in Chapters 5 and 6, numerous new venture companies have been started in Korea throughout the last decades, and many of them are thriving not only domestically, but also internationally. Essentially, the success of these companies is based on Tiger Management as much as that of the well-known *chaebols*. In other words, Tiger Management is applicable to large and small firms alike.

A second issue is family-based ownership and management. Korean companies and business groups tend not only to be owned, but also managed by representatives of their founder families. It can also be said that several features of Tiger Management, such as bold and long-term oriented strategic planning and strong leadership, are significantly supported by such family control. Does this mean that Tiger Management is only relevant for family businesses?

The evidence from Korea suggests the opposite. In recent years, various large state-owned firms such as POSCO and KT (formerly Korea Telecom) were privatized and are now operated as public companies. Therefore, neither the government nor any particular shareholder has a dominant influence over their management. These companies have thrived since privatization and are, in fact, regarded as model companies in their industries.[8] Moreover, their recent success has been built on familiar key features of Tiger Management such as aggressive business planning and strong executive leadership. This clearly shows that Tiger Management can also be successfully adopted by public companies.

Taken together, whereas adopting Tiger Management can be expected to be somewhat more challenging in countries which are culturally distant from Korea than in East Asia, there is no reason to believe that it can be applied only to specific types of companies, such as large business groups or family firms. To the contrary, the evidence from Korea indicates that it is genuine set of managerial practices which can be used by any company, regardless of its size or ownership structure. The essence of Tiger Management will be summarized below, and some important issues related to its adoption process briefly discussed.

Key features of Tiger Management

Tiger Management has many aspects and encompasses various managerial functions, as seen throughout this book. However, the essence of Tiger Management is mostly represented by the following key features:

1. **Entrepreneurial ambition with a long-term perspective**. Tiger entrepreneurs are not satisfied with setting themselves modest goals within the normal range of what competitors are also aiming for. They want to excel by achieving dramatic growth and outstanding results. Their visions often go beyond what is regarded as "common sense" in a market or industry. However, they do not expect to achieve their highly ambitious goals within a quarter or a year. Instead, they plan with a long-term horizon of five, ten, or more years.

2. **Aggressive, risk-taking and persistent business strategies**. In order to achieve their highly ambitious goals, Tiger entrepreneurs invest aggressively and are undeterred by the risk of these investments. They pour all available

human and financial resources into the development of new technologies and the entry into new industries and new markets. They rapidly build new manufacturing sites and distribution networks. They are not afraid of failures and capitalize on them by re-launching their efforts while avoiding previous mistakes. They do not surrender as long as they sense a reasonable chance for eventual success.

3. **Fast implementation.** In Tiger companies, business plans are put into practice with very high speed. Although the companies develop plans with a long-term horizon, they hurry up with implementing them, as it will not be possible to achieve their extremely ambitious goals when their plans are pursued only at a modest pace. Implementation schedules are very tight and will not be moved back. All involved employees will work very intensively to make sure these schedules are kept.

4. **Flexibility regarding implementation methods and approaches.** Whereas Tiger companies are uncompromising regarding implementation schedules, they are undogmatic and flexible regarding the means for how their goals are being achieved. If some specific approach does not work very well, and the perception grows that a different way of solving a task could be more effective, then implementation methods are adjusted very quickly and pragmatically. Nobody resists such changes and sticks to initially formulated ideas, as the fulfillment of business plans and goals on time is regarded as imperative.

5. **Strong executive leadership**. Executives of Tiger companies display strong leadership by actively sharing their highly ambitious business visions with all employees. They excite by envisioning extraordinary goals for their companies and persuade everybody that these goals can really be achieved through a strong collective effort. They motivate and mobilize all employees to work intensively towards making their visions come true. They also lead by their own example and work hard, showing that they believe in their goals, but that exceptional efforts are needed to fulfill them. Through their strong leadership and communication efforts, they pre-empt unproductive and delaying disputes about corporate goals and strategies.

6. **Creating a strong team spirit**. In Tiger companies, a strong spirit of working together is created and cultivated. Leaders and managers emphasize that the company's ambitious goals can only be met through good teamwork. They do not neglect different individual viewpoints and preferences, but induce everybody to work together intensively to achieve the common goals. They also engage in systematic social bonding efforts to help all members familiarize with each other and make them comfortable to work together in a productive team atmosphere.

7. **Emphasis on human skill formation**. The formation of employee skills and capabilities is strongly emphasized in Tiger companies. Applicants' pre-existing skills and their motivation to advance them further are predominant selection criteria when recruiting new employees. Employees do not only work through extensive training programs when they enter the company, but are also trained thereafter on a regular and systematic basis to enhance their professional skills. Tiger companies do not shy away from this high investment into training programs, as they perceive that maximizing their employees' capabilities is pivotal for their business success.

8. **Providing strong motivational incentives**. Finally, Tiger companies also provide strong incentives for their employees to maximize their professional efforts. They offer generous bonus payments on the organizational and individual levels for those units and individuals that contribute strongly to their companies' business results. They also rapidly promote strongly performing employees to higher managerial ranks and thereby reward them financially as well as socially for their accomplishments.

None of these key features of Tiger Management is really new or unknown outside Korea. In fact, many non-Korean companies have already adopted several of these managerial practices. This shows that there is nothing mysterious about Tiger Management, and that it can be basically applied everywhere. It is, however, the combination of these practices that makes Korean companies so successful. They mutually complement each other and thereby constitute a coherent set of managerial tools that prove to be both extremely effective and highly resilient against changes in the business environment.

Managing the adoption process

As none of the key features of Tiger Management is in itself particularly difficult to understand, non-Korean companies interested in adopting it could, in principle, rely on descriptions of Korean management practices to study and adopt it. However, transfer experiences with other comprehensive managerial concepts, such as lean production, have shown that this approach may not be sufficient for an effective knowledge transfer across organizations, particularly on an international level. Western observers began to study best practices from their Japanese counterparts from the late 1970s, and detailed descriptions of lean production and lean management were available in the English language from around 1990.[9] However, it took even those non-Japanese firms who were very eager to study it at least another decade to implement it successfully in their own organizations. In the process, they typically interacted directly with Japanese companies to understand and absorb the essence of their management systems in practice.[10]

Given these experiences, it appears most promising for non-Korean companies with a serious interest in Tiger Management to study it intensively via direct interaction with leading Korean companies. Many companies already have direct ties with Korean firms through business and technology alliances. Not all Korean companies may be equally open to share their knowledge with others. However, some among them are in fact quite eager to exchange best managerial practices with leading Western firms mutually. Moreover, in contrast to many pieces of technological knowledge, managerial practices can be often be understood to a fair extent through direct observation. In other words, even without a formal benchmarking or transfer process, non-Korean companies may be able to improve their understanding of Tiger Management by observing their Korean business partners when working together.

Regardless of the specific channel of knowledge transfer chosen by a company, however, several managerial policies should be applied to maximize the effectiveness of the adoption process of Tiger Management.[11] First, specific goals of knowledge transfer should be defined in advance. Ideally, these goals are measurable in terms of business performance metrics, such as shorter implementation cycles of new products. In case the direct measurement by performance indicators proves to be difficult, it is still helpful to define specific goals regarding the adoption of managerial practices, such as teamwork or training programs. If there are no clearly defined goals, it is likely that the whole transfer process becomes diluted and ineffective.

Second, cultural differences between Korea and the target country need to be taken into consideration, as mentioned earlier. If these differences are large, there is a high possibility that certain features of Tiger Management need to be adapted to the cultural context of the target country. For example, in Western countries with strong egalitarian traditions, strong leadership may need to be implemented in different ways from Korea, or other East Asian countries with a strong Confucian influence. Executives may need to emphasize the logical stringency of their plans more strongly in Western countries to persuade employees that they are viable. Such local adaption does not mean, however, that the essence of Tiger Management cannot be transferred to different countries and cultures. As shown in Chapters 10 and 11, Korean companies adapted Tiger Management successfully to different and changing contexts, both at home and abroad.

Third, project managers or implementation managers should be assigned and given the necessary authority within the specific task to see through the knowledge transfer and adoption of managerial practices. As discussed earlier in this chapter, there are many potential obstacles to such international transfer of management knowledge, and organizational resistance at the receiving side is likely to occur at some point. Therefore, the existence of managers who can persuade everyone of the value and importance of the transfer process, and ensure the implementation of managerial practices, is pivotal for their effective adoption.

Conclusion

Korean companies have been tremendously successful throughout the last fifty years. Their achievements cover a wide range of industries and are visible almost anywhere in the world. From this viewpoint, business executives should be universally interested in understanding the best managerial practices named Tiger Management in this book.

It could still be argued that Tiger Management may be more effective in certain contexts than in others. Its implementation can be expected to be more challenging in countries which are culturally distant from Korea than in others which are more similar. Moreover, some features of Tiger Management may have a particularly good fit with the business environment in certain countries and industries. Aggressive business planning, speed, and flexibility appear to be especially effective in the volatile and dynamic environments of emerging markets and in high tech industries that are subject to frequent disruption and innovation. However, it is also evident that emerging markets now play a leading role in the growth of the world economy, and that from groundbreaking innovations in information and communication technologies, a wide range of industries is now much more dynamic than it used to be even a few decades ago. In other words, various global megatrends make Tiger Management ever more attractive from a business perspective. This also helps to explain why Korean companies are so significantly successful not only in their home country, but also globally.

The bottom line of this book is, therefore, that Tiger Management deserves broad global attention. Business executives around the world should study it not only to understand their Korean competitors, but also to consider seriously what can be learned from them.

Notes

1 Tiger management

1 Michael Bourne's book *Thoth: Where the Paranormal meets Mind*. Korean Mythology. Available online: http://www.book-of-thoth.com/thebook/index.php/Korean_mythology#The_Sun_and_the_Moon (accessed 7 November 2011).

2 For example, E. Vogel, *Japan as Number One: Lessons for America*, Cambridge, MA: Harvard University Press, 1979; and J. C. Abegglen and G. Stalk, *Kaisha: the Japanese Corporation*, New York: Basic Books, 1985.

3 For example, M.-J. Chen, *Inside Chinese Business: A Guide for Managers Worldwide*, Boston: Harvard Business School Press, 2001; and T. Plafker, *Doing Business in China: How to Profit in the World's Fastest Growing Market*, New York: Warner Business Books, 2007.

4 A. Amsden, *Asia's Next Giant: South Korea and Late Industrialization*, New York and Oxford: Oxford University Press, 1989.

5 G. R. Ungson, R. M. Steers, and S.-H. Park, *Korean Enterprise: The Quest for Globalization*, Boston: Harvard Business School Press, 1997.

6 For example, S.-H. Jwa and I. K. Lee (eds), "Introduction" in *Korean Chaebol in Transition: Road Ahead and Agenda*, Seoul: Korea Economic Research Institute, 2000, 17–34; C. Rowley, J. Bae, and T. W. Sohn, "Introduction: Capabilities to Liabilities in Korean Management" in C. Rowley, T.-W. Sohn, and J. Bae (eds), *Managing Korean Business: Organization, Culture, Human Resources and Change*, London: Frank Cass, 2002, 1–21; S.-J. Chang, *Financial Crisis and Transformation of Korean Business Groups: The Rise and Fall of Chaebols*, Cambridge: Cambridge University Press, 2003.

7 For example, V. Pucik and J.-C. Lim, "Transforming Human Resource Management in a Korean Chaebol: A Case Study of Samsung" in C. Rowley, T.-W. Sohn, and J. Bae (eds), *Managing Korean Business: Organization, Culture, Human Resources and Change*, London: Frank Cass, 2002, 137–60; S. Choe and T. Roehl, "What to Shed and What to Keep: Corporate Transformation in Korean Business Groups," *Long Range Planning*, 2007, 40(4–5): 465–87; K. Lee, M. W. Peng, and K. Lee, "From Diversification Premium to Diversification Discount during Institutional Transitions," *Journal of World Business*, 2008, 43(1): 47–65.

8 E. M. Kim, *The Four Asian Tigers: Economic Development and the Global Political Economy,* San Diego: Academic Press, 1998.

9 M. Hobday, *Innovation in East Asia: The Challenge to Japan*, Cheltenham: Edward Elgar, 1995, 1.

10 A.-L. Allen and J. Holt, *Exploring North-East Asia: China, Japan*, Korea, Carlton: Curriculum, 1999, 4.

11 J. S. Shin and S.-W. Jang, *Creating First-Mover Advantages: The Case of Samsung Electronics*, SCAPE Working Paper No. 2005/13, Department of Economics, National University of Singapore, 2005, 3.

12 Gartner, "Gartner Says 428 Million Mobile Communication Devices Sold Worldwide in First Quarter 2011, a 19 Percent Increase Year-on-Year." Press Release, 19 May 2011. Available online: http://www.gartner.com/it/page.jsp?id=1689814 (accessed 10 November 2011).

13 LG Electronics, Korea Invest Forum Presentation. Available online: http://www.lg.com/global/ir/reports/other-presentations.jsp (accessed 7 November 2011).

14 OICA - International Organization of Motor Vehicle Manufacturers, World Ranking of Manufacturers, Year 2010. Available online: http://oica.net/wp-content/uploads/ranking-2010.pdf (accessed 7 November 2011).

15 IISI – World Steel Association, World Steel Top Producers 2010. Available online: http://www.worldsteel.org/statistics/top-producers.html (accessed 7 November 2011).

16 I. Moon, "Korea's Shipbuilding Industry Sails Ahead," *Business Week*, 12 May 2006.

17 SAJ – The Shipbuilders' Association of Japan, Shipbuilding Statistics, September 2011. Available online: http://www.sajn.or.jp/e/statistics/Shipbuilding_Statistics_Sep2011e.pdf (accessed 7 November 2011).

18 R. Hassink and D.-H. Shin, "South Korea's Shipbuilding Industry: From a Couple of Cathedrals in the Desert to an Innovative Cluster," *Asian Journal of Technology Innovation*, 2005, 13(2): 146–51.

19 Samsung Electronics, Annual Report 2010. Available online: http://www.samsung.com/us/aboutsamsung/ir/financialinformation/annualreport/downloads/2010/SECAR2010_Eng_Final.pdf (accessed 7 November 2011).

20 Small and Medium Business Administration, Survey Statistics System. Available online: http://stat2.smba.go.kr/dbsearch_re_01.jsp (accessed 7 November 2011). 중소기업청, 조사통계시스템.

21 Korea IT Times, "30 Korean Software Companies Worthy of Global Recognition in 2012," 15 July 2011.

22 Economist, "South Korea's Pop-cultural Exports: Hallyu, Yeah! A 'Korean Wave' Washes Warmly over Asia," 25 January 2010.

23 Bank of Korea, Economic Statistics System. Available online: http://ecos.bok.or.kr/EIndex_en.jsp (accessed 7 November 2011).

2 The seeds of Tiger Management

1 H.-J. Jin, "Lee Byung-chull: the Man who Founded the Samsung Empire," *Korea Herald*, 30 March 2010.

2 D. Kirk, *Korean Dynasty: Hyundai and Chung Ju Yung*, Armonk, NY: Sharpe, 1994, 39.

3 C. Hur, "Culture, Goal-Oriented Communication (Leadership), and a Fast Growing Organization: the Case of Samsung Electronics," 21. Available online: http://www.ad.co.kr/lit/report/download.xhr?objectType=LR&objectUkey=3423&fileName=3423.pdf (accessed 7 November 2011).

4 C. J. Kim, *The History of Korea*, Westport, CT: Greenwood Press, 2005, 91.

5 T. K. Oh, "Understanding Managerial Values and Behavior Among the Gang of Four: South Korea, Taiwan, Singapore and Hong Kong," in *Journal of Management Development*, 1991, 10(2): 46–56.

6 G. Hofstede, *Culture's Consequences*, 2nd ed., Thousand Oaks: Sage, 2001, 87.

7 T. K. Oh and E. Kim, "The Impact of Confucianism on East Asian Business Enterprises," in Z. Rhee and E. Chang (eds), *Korean Business and Management: the Reality and the Vision,* Elizabeth, NJ: Hollym, 2002, 213–4.

8 Oh and Kim, "The Impact of Confucianism on East Asian Business Enterprises", 213.

9 I. K. Kim, "Confucian Culture and Economic Development: Focusing on Korea and Japan," *Hanil Kyeongsang Nonsip*, 1984, 1(0): 13–5. 김일곤, 유교문화권(儒教文

化圈)의 경제발전(經濟發展) –한국(韓國)과 일본(日本)을 중심(中心)으로-, 한
일경상논집.
10 Y.-H. Cho and J. Yoon, "The Origin and Function of Dynamic Collectivism: An
Analysis of Korean Corporate Culture," *Asia Pacific Business Review*, 2001, 7(4):
74–5, 79–80.
11 Kim, *The History of Korea*, 119–39.
12 A. Amsden, *Asia's Next Giant: South Korea and Late Industrialization*, New York and
Oxford: Oxford University Press, 1989, 30–1.
13 Amsden, *Asia's Next Giant*, 31.
14 P. Francks, *Japanese Economic Development*, 2nd ed., London: Routledge, 1999,
29–41.
15 H. Lee, *Economic History of Korea*, 2nd ed., Seoul: Beobmunsa, 1999, 273–89. 이헌창,
한국경제통사, 제2판, 서울: 법문사.
16 Lee, *Economic History of Korea*, 319–49.
17 Kim, *The History of Korea*, 138.
18 E. M. Kim, *Big Business, Strong State: Collusion and Conflict in South Korean
Development, 1960–1990*, Albany: State University of New York Press, 1997, 90–1.
19 Lee, *Economic History of Korea*, 376–91.
20 Amsden, *Asia's Next Giant*, 39.
21 D.-S. Cho, "From Subsidizer to Regulator – The Changing Role of Korean Government," *Long Range Planning*, 1992, 25(6): 51.
22 Amsden, *Asia's Next Giant*, 42, 48–9.
23 S.-J. Chang, *Financial Crisis and Transformation of Korean Business Groups: The
Rise and Fall of Chaebols*, Cambridge: Cambridge University Press, 2003, 4–8.
24 Kim, *Big Business, Strong State*, 40.
25 M. L. Clifford, *Troubled Tiger: Businessmen, Bureaucrats, and Generals in South
Korea*, Armond, NY: Sharpe, 1998, 47–53.

3 Rising Tigers

1 R. M. Steers, *Made in Korea: Chung Ju Yung and the Rise of Hyundai*, New York and
London: Routledge, 1999, 1.
2 C. J. Eckert, *Offspring of Empire: The Koch'ang Kims and the Colonial Origins of
Korean Capitalism 1876–1945*, Seattle and London: University of Washington Press,
1991, 27–8.
3 D. S. Juhn, "The Development of Korean Entrepreneurship," in A. C. Nahm (ed.),
Korea Under Japanese Colonial Rule, Center for Korean Studies, Western Michigan
University, 1973, 115.
4 A. Amsden, *Asia's Next Giant: South Korea and Late Industrialization*, New York and
Oxford: Oxford University Press, 1989, 34.
5 Juhn, "The Development of Korean Entrepreneurship," 118–20.
6 H. Lee, *Economic History of Korea*, 2nd ed., Seoul: Beobmunsa, 1999, 353–5. 이헌창,
한국경제통사, 제2판, 서울: 법문사.
7 D. Mcnamara, "The Keishō and the Korean Business Elite," *Journal of Asian Studies*,
1989, 48(2): 311–8.
8 Juhn, "The Development of Korean Entrepreneurship," 127.
9 Lee, *Economic History of Korea*, 334.
10 Juhn, "The Development of Korean Entrepreneurship," 122–31.
11 Eckert, *Offspring of Empire*, 29–37; Mcnamara, "The Keishō and the Korean Business
Elite," 312–8.
12 D.-S. Cho, *Research on Korean Business Groups*, rev. ed., Seoul: Maeil Kyeongjae
Sinmunsa, 1991, 158. 조동성, 한국재벌연구, 개정1판, 서울: 매일경제신문사.
13 S.-J. Chang, *Financial Crisis and Transformation of Korean Business Groups: The
Rise and Fall of Chaebols*, Cambridge: Cambridge University Press, 2003, 46.

14 D.-S. Cho, "From Subsidizer to Regulator – The Changing Role of Korean Government," *Long Range Planning*, 1992, 25(6): 51.
15 Amsden, *Asia's Next Giant*, 39.
16 Cho, "From Subsidizer to Regulator," 51.
17 Amsden, *Asia's Next Giant*, 40.
18 M. Kuk, "The Governmental Role in the Making of Chaebol in the Industrial Development of South Korea," *Asian Perspective*, 1988, 12(1): 112.
19 Cho, *Research on Korean Business Groups*, 166.
20 Chang, *Financial Crisis and Transformation of Korean Business Groups*, 47.
21 Kim, *Big Business, Strong State: Collusion and Conflict in South Korean Development, 1960–1990*, Albany: State University of New York Press, 1997, 82–4.
22 Chang, *Financial Crisis and Transformation of Korean Business Groups*, 54.
23 Kim, *Big Business, Strong State*, 98–101.
24 Chang, *Financial Crisis and Transformation of Korean Business Groups*, 49–50.
25 Statistics Agency Korea, *Change of the Korean Economy and Society over 50 years from a Statistical Viewpoint*, Seoul: Statistics Agency, 1998, 116. 통계로 본 대한민국 50년의 경제사회상 변화, 서울: 통계청.
26 Chang, *Financial Crisis and Transformation of Korean Business Groups*, 50–1.
27 Detailed information regarding Samsung Group can be found in Samsung Chairman Secretariat Office, *60 Year History of Samsung*, Seoul: Samsung Chairman Secretariat Office, 1998. 삼성회장비서실, 삼성60년사, 서울: 삼성회장비서실.
28 Detailed information regarding Hyundai Group can be found in D. Kirk, *Korean Dynasty: Hyundai and Chung Ju Yung*, Armonk, NY: Sharpe, 1994; and Steers, *Made in Korea*, 1999.
29 Steers, *Made in Korea*, 95.
30 Detailed information regarding LG Group can be found in LG Corporation, *Passion for Customers, Challenging the Future: 60 Year History of LG*, 2007. 주식회사LG, 고객에대한 열정, 미래를 향한도전, 서울: 주식회사LG.
31 Detailed information regarding SK Group can be found in SK Corporate Culture Office, *A Journey of Ambition and Intelligence: 50 Years of SK*, Seoul: SK Corporate Culture Office, 2006. SK기업문화실, 패기와 지성의 여정: SK 50년, 서울: SK기업 문화실.
32 Detailed information regarding Daewoo Group can be found in Daewoo Global Management Research Study Group, *30 Year History of Daewoo*, Seoul: Daewoo Global Management Research Study Group, 2010. 대우세계경영연구회, 대우30년사, 서울: 대우세계경영연구회.
33 Chang, *Financial Crisis and Transformation of Korean Business Groups*, 91–8.
34 Y.-I. Chung, "Chaebol Entrepreneurs in the Early Stage of Korean Economic Development," *Journal of Modern Korean Studies*, 1985, 2 (Dec): 20.

4　Globalizing Tigers

1 R. M. Steers, *Made in Korea: Chung Ju Yung and the Rise of Hyundai*, New York and London: Routledge, 1999, 111.
2 Steers, *Made in Korea*, 109.
3 C. W. Kang, "An analysis of Japanese Policy and Economic Change in Korea," in A. C. Nahm (ed.), *Korea Under Japanese Colonial Rule*, Center for Korean Studies, Western Michigan University, 1973, 84–5.
4 H. Lee, *Economic History of Korea*, 2nd ed., Seoul: Beobmunsa, 1999, 444. 이헌창, 한국경제통사, 제2판, 서울: 법문사.
5 R. M. Steers, Y. K. Shin and G. R. Ungson, *The Chaebol: Korea's New Industrial Might*, New York: Ballinger, 1989, 76.
6 A. Amsden, *Asia's Next Giant: South Korea and Late Industrialization*, New York and Oxford: Oxford University Press, 1989, 41.

7 Steers, *Made in Korea*, 83.
8 D. Kirk, *Korean Dynasty: Hyundai and Chung Ju Yung*, Armonk, NY: Sharpe, 1994, 136.
9 Steers, *Made in Korea*, 82.
10 Steers, *Made in Korea*, 80.
11 M. L. Clifford, *Troubled Tiger: Businessmen, Bureaucrats, and Generals in South Korea*, 2nd ed., Armond: Sharpe, 1998, 256.
12 Daewoo Global Management Research Study Group, *30 Year History of Daewoo*, Seoul: Daewoo Global Management Research Study Group, 2010, 19–20. 대우세계경영연구회, 대우 30년사, 서울: 대우세계경영연구회.
13 Daewoo Global Management Research Study Group, *30 Year History of Daewoo*, 17.
14 Daewoo Global Management Research Study Group, *30 Year History of Daewoo*, 18.
15 D.-S. Cho, *Research on Korean Business Groups*, rev. ed., Seoul: Maeil Kyeongjae Sinmunsa, 1991, 249. 조동성, 한국재벌연구, 개정1판, 서울: 매일경제신문사.
16 Samsung Chairman Secretariat Office, *60 Year History of Samsung*, Seoul: Samsung Chairman Secretariat Office, 1998, 66–7. 삼성회장비서실, 삼성60년사, 서울: 삼성회장비서실.
17 Steers, Shin, and Ungson, *The Chaebol*, 80–2.
18 J. S. Shin and S.-W. Jang, *Creating First-Mover Advantages: The Case of Samsung Electronics*, SCAPE Working Paper No. 2005/13, Department of Economics, National University of Singapore, 2005, 9–11.
19 Shin and Jang, *Creating First-Mover Advantages*, 8–19.
20 Cho, *Research on Korean Business Groups*, 227.
21 Steers, *Made in Korea*, 64.
22 Steers, *Made in Korea*, 111–7.
23 Kirk, *Korean Dynasty*, 75–6.
24 Daewoo Global Management Research Study Group, *30 Year History of Daewoo*, 108–9.
25 Kirk, *Korean Dynasty*, 145.
26 Kirk, *Korean Dynasty*, 147.
27 R. D. Lansbury, C.-S. Suh, and S. H. Kwon, *The Global Korean Motor Industry: The Hyundai Motor Company's Global Strategy*, New York: Routledge, 2007, 54.
28 Samsung Chairman Secretariat Office, *60 Year History of Samsung*, 142–5.
29 Samsung Chairman Secretariat Office, *60 Year History of Samsung*, 308–11.
30 LG Corporation, *Passion for Customers, Challenging the Future: 60 Year History of LG*, 2007, 170. 주식회사LG, 고객에 대한 열정, 미래를 향한도전, 서울: 주식회사LG.
31 Daewoo Global Management Research Study Group, *30 Year History of Daewoo*, 288.

5 Struggling Tigers

1 Principal Voices round-table, Beijing, 16 May 2005. Available online: http://www.principalvoices.com/beijing.html (accessed 12 November 2011).
2 Representative publications include C. S. Chang and N. J. Chang, *The Korean Management System: Cultural, Political, Economic Foundations*, Westport, CN: Quorum, 1994; K. H. Chung, H. C. Lee, and J. H. Jung, *Korean Management: Global Strategy and Cultural Transformation*, Berlin: Walter de Gruyter, 1997; and G. R. Ungson, R. M. Steers, and S.-H. Park, *Korean Enterprise: The Quest for Globalization*, Boston: Harvard Business School Press, 1997.
3 Y. Iwasaki, "Wither Thailand?" in W. C. Hunter, G. G. Kaufman, and T. H. Krueger (eds), *The Asian Financial Crisis: Origins, Implications, and Solutions*, Boston: Kluwer, 1999, 194–5.
4 Y.-D. Euh and J. H. Rhee, "Lessons from the Korean Crisis: Policy and Managerial Implications," *Long Range Planning*, 2007, 40(4/5): 437.
5 S.-J. Chang, *Financial Crisis and Transformation of Korean Business Groups: The Rise and Fall of Chaebols*, Cambridge: Cambridge University Press, 2003, 3.

6 Bank of Korea, Economic Statistics System. Available online: http://ecos.bok.or.kr/EIndex_en.jsp (accessed 12 November 2011).
7 Euh and Rhee, "Lessons from the Korean Crisis", 436.
8 Chang, *Financial Crisis and Transformation of Korean Business Groups,* 141.
9 Chang, *Financial Crisis and Transformation of Korean Business Groups,* 154.
10 W. Lee and N. S. Lee, "Understanding Samsung's Diversification Strategy: The Case of Samsung Motors Inc," *Long Range Planning,* 2007, 40(4/5): 490–1.
11 W.-S. Shim and R. M. Steers, "The Entrepreneurial Basis of Korean Enterprise: Past Accomplishments and Future Challenges," *Asia Pacific Business Review,* 2001, 7(4): 35–6.
12 D.-J. Kim, "Falls from Grace and Lessons from Failure: Daewoo and Medison," *Long Range Planning,* 2007, 40(4/5): 449–52.
13 Chang, *Financial Crisis and Transformation of Korean Business Groups,* 190–1.
14 K. Lee and C. H. Lee, "The Miracle to Crisis and the Mirage of the Postcrisis Reform in Korea: Assessment after Ten Years," *Journal of Asian Economics,* 2008, 19(5/6): 432.
15 Chang, *Financial Crisis and Transformation of Korean Business Groups,* 202.
16 Chang, *Financial Crisis and Transformation of Korean Business Groups,* 203–4.
17 Chang, *Financial Crisis and Transformation of Korean Business Groups,* 204–8.
18 S. Choe and T. W. Roehl, "What to Shed and What to Keep: Corporate Transformation in Korean Business Groups," *Long Range Planning,* 2007, 40(4/5): 469.
19 S. Choe and C. Pattnaik, "The Transformation of Korean Business Groups after the Asian Crisis," *Journal of Contemporary Asia,* 2007, 37(2): 243.
20 H. Kim, R. E. Hoskisson, L. Tihanyi, and J. Hong, "The Evolution of Diversified Business Groups in Emerging Markets: the Lessons from Chaebols in Korea," *Asia Pacific Journal of Management,* 2004, 21(1): 42.
21 Choe and Roehl, "What to Shed and What to Keep," 484.
22 Choe and Pattnaik, "The Transformation of Korean Business Groups after the Asian Crisis," 236–9.
23 LG Corporation, *Passion for Customers, Challenging the Future,* 237–9.
24 S.-J. Chang, "Business Groups in East Asia: Post-crisis Restructuring and New Growth," *Asia Pacific Journal of Management,* 2006, 23(4): 413–4.
25 Choe and Pattnaik, "The Transformation of Korean Business Groups after the Asian Crisis," 244–50.
26 See, for example, the strongly different assessments given by Choe and Pattnaik, "The Transformation of Korean Business Groups after the Asian Crisis," 251–2, and O. Y. Kwon, *The Korean Economy in Transition: An Institutional Perspective*, Cheltenham: Edward Elgar, 2010, 229–30, regarding this issue.
27 See, for example, LG Corporation, *Passion for Customers, Challenging the Future,* 231–9 regarding reorganization measures implemented in various LG group companies.
28 C. Rowley and J. Bae, "Globalization and Transformation of Human Resource Management in South Korea," *International Journal of Human Resource Management,* 2002, 13(3): 540.
29 V. Pucik and J.-C. Lim, "Transforming Human Resource Management in a Korean Chaebol: A Case Study of Samsung," *Asia Pacific Business Review,* 2001, 7(4): 156–7.
30 S. H. Chon, S. O. Park, S. M. Oh, and J. S. Park, *Outsourcing Strategy of ReignCom, the MP3 Corporation*, KAIST Case Competition, Seoul, 2004, 3.
31 T. Hussain, *Diamond Dilemma: Shaping Korea for the 21st Century*, Seoul, 2006, 112–3.
32 Ahnlab, About Ahnlab: Overview. Available online: http://www.ahnlab.com/company/site/eng/about/overview.jsp (accessed 12 November 2011).

6 Revitalized Tigers

1 Samsung Electronics, *40 Years of Samsung Electronics: the Legacy of Challenge and Creativity*, Suwon: Samsung Electronics Corp., 2010, 172. 삼성전자주식회사: 삼성전자 40년: 도전과창조의 유산, 수원: 삼성전자주식회사. Author's translation.

2 Bank of Korea, *Financial Statement Analysis for 2009*, Seoul: Bank of Korea, 2010.
3 S.-J. Chang, *Sony vs. Samsung: The Inside Story of the Electronics Giants' Battle for Global Supremacy*, Singapore: Wiley, 2008, 94–5.
4 K. Lee and X. He, "The Capability of the Samsung Group in Project Execution and Vertical Integration: Created in Korea, Replicated in China," *Asian Business and Management*, 2009, 8(3): 284–91.
5 Lee and He, 'The Capability of the Samsung Group in Project Execution and Vertical Integration', 291–5.
6 A. Michell, *Samsung Electronics and the Struggle for Leadership in the Electronics Industry*, Singapore: Wiley, 2010, 93–101.
7 Interbrand, Best Global Brands 2010. Available online: http://www.interbrand.com/ko/best-global-brands/best-global-brands-2008/best-global-brands-2010.aspx (accessed 13 November 2011).
8 IFI Claims Patent Services, IFI Claims Announces Top Global Companies Ranked By 2010 U.S. Patents. Available online: http://www.ificlaims.com/news/top-patents.html (accessed 13 November 2011).
9 K. J. Freeze and K.-W. Chung, *Epilogue March 2008: What Actually Happened at Samsung Design*, Case Study DMI023. Boston, MA: Design Management Institute, 2008, 3.
10 Samsung Electronics, Annual Report 2010, 84. Available online: http://www.samsung.com/us/aboutsamsung/ir/financialinformation/annualreport/downloads/2010/SECAR2010_Eng_Final.pdf (accessed 7 November 2011).
11 M. Chacksfield, "Samsung Becomes the World's Biggest Technology Company. HP Drops to Second Place," *World of Tech News*, 29 January 2010. Available online: http://www.techradar.com/news/world-of-tech/samsung-becomes-the-world-s-biggest-technology-company-667152 (accessed 13 November 2011).
12 R. D. Lansbury, C.-S. Suh, and S.-H. Kwon, *The Global Korean Motor Industry*, Oxford: Routledge, 2007, 44.
13 B.-H. Lee and S.-J. Cho, "Merger and Reconfiguring of Hyundai-Kia," paper presented at ninth GERPISA International Conference, Paris, 2001, 7–13. Available online: http://gerpisa.org/rencontre/9.rencontre/S13Lee-Cho.pdf (accessed 2 December 2011).
14 Maeil Business, 'Putin personally Congratulates at Opening Ceremony of Hyundai Motor's Factory in Russia', 24 September 2010. 푸틴이 직접축하한 현대차 공장 준공식, 매일경제.
15 KBS World, "Hyundai Kia Overseas Production to Top 50% Next Year," 11 November 2010. Available online: http://world.kbs.co.kr/english/news/news_Ec_detail.htm?No=77104 (accessed 13 November 2011).
16 H. J. Jo and J.-S. You, "Transferring Production Systems: An Institutionalist Account of Hyundai Motor Company in the United States," *Journal of East Asian Studies*, 2011, 11(1): 42.
17 Chosun Ilbo, "Hyundai Kia, after China, India, and Europe, Now Also Overtaking Japanese in South America, only North America Remaining," 4 July 2011. 현대 기아, 中, 印, 유럽 이어 南美서 日추월, 北美만남아, 조선일보.
18 Hankook Kyungjae, "Hyundai Kia Motor Breaking for the First Time Through 10% Market Share in US market," 7 June 2011. 현대 기아차, 美 시장 점유율 첫 10% 돌파, 한국경제.
19 Jo and You, "Transferring Production Systems", 50.
20 K. Lee, C. Lim, and W. Song, "Emerging Digital Technology as a Window of Opportunity and Technological Leapfrogging," *International Journal of Technology Management*, 2005, 29(1/2): 52–6.
21 J. R. Lee and M. Shin, *International Business*, 3rd ed., Seoul: Hongmoonsa, 2008, 5. 이장로, 신만수, 국제경영, 제3판, 서울:홍문사.
22 S.-H. Kwon, D.-K. Rhee, and C.-S. Suh, "Globalization Strategies of South Korean Electronics Companies After the 1997 Asian Financial Crisis," *Asia Pacific Business Review*, 2004, 10(3/4): 432.

23 Y. Park, J. Shintaku, J. Tomita, P. Hong, and G. Moon, "Modularity of Flat Panel Display TV and Operation Management Practices: A Case Study of LG Electronics," MMRC Discussion Paper Series No. 248, Tokyo: Manufacturing Management Research Center, 2009, 12–18.

24 A. Inkpen and K. Ramaswamy, "End of the Multinational: Emerging Markets Redraw the Picture," *Journal of Business Strategy*, 2007, 28(5): 4.

25 Hankook Kyungjae, "LG Electronics Overseas Campaign: Now Africa," 20 June 2008. LG전자 해외공략 '이젠 아프리카다', 한국경제.

26 LG Electronics, Company Overview, 2010 Brochure. Available online: http://www.lg.com/global/ir/company-information/overview.jsp (accessed 13 November 2011).

27 Korea Times, "Venture firm Humax Finally Thriving," 31 January 2011.

28 Humax, Milestones. Available online: http://www.humaxdigital.com/global/abouthumax/milestones.asp (accessed 13 November 2011).

29 Korea Times, "Venture firm Humax Finally Thriving."

30 AhnLab, About AhnLab: Introduction of Founder. Available online: http://www.ahn-lab.com/company/site/about/founder_retire.jsp (accessed 13 November 2011). About AhnLab: 설립자소개.

31 AhnLab, About AhnLab: Overview. Available online: http://www.ahnlab.com/company/site/eng/about/overview.jsp (accessed 13 November 2011).

32 Korea IT Times, "AhnLab Considers Overseas M&A," 22 October 2009.

33 T. Hussain, *Diamond Dilemma: Shaping Korea for the 21st Century*, Seoul, 2006, 114.

34 NCsoft, About Us: History. Available online: http://global.ncsoft.com/global/aboutus/milestone.aspx (accessed 14 November 2011).

35 NCsoft, IR Presentation September 2011. Available online: http://global.ncsoft.com/global/board/downloadlist.aspx?BID=ir_pr (accessed 14 November 2011).

36 SM Entertainment, About Us. Available online: http://www.smtown.com/ir/main.aspx (accessed 14 November 2011).

37 H. Peng, The History of SM Entertainment's Growing Empire. Youth Voices. Available online: http://youthvoices.net/discussion/history-sm-entertainments-growing-empire (accessed 14 November 2011).

38 Chosun Ilbo, "Adding One Subsidiary Every Three Days… Half of the 'Octopus Legs' Lose money," 22 June 2011. "사흘에 하나씩 계열사 늘려… '문어발의 성적' 절반이 적자", 조선일보.

7 Tiger strategy

1 Samsung Electronics, *40 Years of Samsung Electronics: the Legacy of Challenge and Creativity*, Suwon: Samsung Electronics Corp., 254. 삼성전자주식회사: 삼성전자 40년: 도전과창조의 유산, 수원: 삼성전자주식회사. Author's translation.

2 Lotte Group, Business Areas. Available online: http://www.lotte.co.kr/english/s2_business/businessarea.html (accessed 15 November 2011).

3 Hanwha Group, Overview. Available online: http://www.hanwha.co.kr/english/index.jsp (accessed 15 November 2011).

4 Kumho Asiana Group, Group Overview. Available online: http://www.kumhoasiana.com/kumho_en /SubMain.asp?pgm_id=KUMHO000003 (accessed 15 November 2011).

5 OECD, *Main Science and Technology Indicators*, Paris: OECD Publishing, 2011, 47, 49. The only countries with higher R&D expenditure ratios are the small, technology intensive economies of Sweden, Finland, and Israel.

6 OECD, *Main Science and Technology Indicators*, 89.

7 L. Kim, *Imitation to Innovation: The Dynamics of Korea's Technological Learning*, Boston: Harvard Business School Press, 1997, 135–46.

8 Samsung Electronics, The R&D Workforce & Organization. Available online: http://www.samsung.com/hk_en/aboutsamsung/companyprofile/researchanddevelopment/CompanyProfile_RD_WorkforceOrganization.html (accessed 5 September 2011).

9 Samsung Electronics, Global R&D Network. Available online: http:/ /www.samsung. com/hk_en/aboutsamsung/companyprofile/researchanddevelopment/CompanyProfile_ Global_RD_Network.html (accessed 21 September 2011).

10 LG Electronics, About LG: LG's Innovative R&D Efforts Reflect "Your Dreams." Available online: http://www.lgcommercial.eu/about-lg (accessed 21 September 2011).

11 Hankook Kyungjae, "LG Electronics Says Solar Batteries will Grow TV and Cellular Phone Business in 10 years," 11 March 2010. "LG 전자 '태양전지, 10년후 TV, 휴대 폰만큼 커진다", 한국경제.

12 Hankook Kyungjae, "Hyundai Motor Shows Next Generation Hybrid for the First Time in Germany," 14 September 2009. "현대차, 차세대 하이브리드 독서 첫공개", 한국경제.

13 Hankook Kyungjae, "LG Electronic's International Campaign now Focusing on Africa," 20 June 2008. LG 전자 해외공략 "이젠 아프리카다", 한국경제.

14 R. M. Steers, *Made in Korea: Chung Ju Yung and the Rise of Hyundai*, New York and London: Routledge, 1999, 75.

15 Steers, *Made in Korea*, 81.

16 L. Kim, *Imitation to Innovation: The Dynamics of Korea's Technological Learning*, Boston: Harvard Business School Press, 1997, 153–5; J. Lee and J. Slater, "Dynamic Capabilities, Entrepreneurial Rent-seeking and the Investment Development Path: The case of Samsung," *Journal of International Management*, 2007, 13(3): 248.

17 J. S. Shin and S.-W. Jang, *Creating First-Mover Advantages: The Case of Samsung Electronics*, SCAPE Working Paper No. 2005/13, Department of Economics, National University of Singapore, 2005, 12–3.

18 Y.-H. Cho and J. Yoon, "The Origin and Function of Dynamic Collectivism: An Analysis of Korean Corporate Culture," *Asia Pacific Business Review*, 2001, 7(4): 81.

19 Shin and Jang, *Creating First-Mover Advantages,* 13–4.

20 Maeil Business, "Analyzing Samsung's Five Future Growth Businesses," 12 May 2010. "삼성, 5개 신수종사업 들여다 보니", 매일경제.

21 Steers, *Made in Korea*, 76–80.

22 Kim, *Imitation to Innovation*, 134–5.

23 LG Corporation, *Passion for Customers, Challenging the Future: 60 Year History of LG*, 2007, 213. 주식회사LG,고객에대한 열정, 미래를 향한도전, 서울: 주식회사LG.

24 Steers, *Made in Korea*, 110.

25 Steers, *Made in Korea*, 81.

26 S.-J. Chang, *Financial Crisis and Transformation of Korean Business Groups: The Rise and Fall of Chaebols*, Cambridge: Cambridge University Press, 2003, 87–91.

8 Tiger leadership

1 Daewoo Global Management Research Association, *30 Year History of Daewoo*, Seoul: Daewoo Global Management Research Association, 2010, 264. 대우세계경영연구원: 대우 30년사, 서울: 대우세계경영연구회. Author's translation.

2 Economist, "South Korea's Industrial Giants: Return of the Overlord," 31 March 2010.

3 See, for example, P. W. Dorfman, J. P. Howell, S. Hibino, J. K. Lee, U. Tate, and A. Bautista, "Leadership in Western and Asian countries: Commonalities and Differences in Effective Leadership Processes across Cultures," *Leadership Quarterly*, 1997, 8(3): 239–40; and D.-J. Kim, "Falls from Grace and Lessons from Failure: Daewoo and Medison," *Long Range Planning*, 2007, 40(4/5): 448, 453.

4 Samsung Electronics, *40 Years of Samsung Electronics: the Legacy of Challenge and Creativity*, Suwon: Samsung Electronics Corp., 11. 삼성전자주식회사: 삼성전자 40년: 도전과창조의 유산, 수원: 삼성전자주식회사.

5 R. M. Steers, *Made in Korea, Chung Ju Yung and the Rise of Hyundai*, New York and London: Routledge, 1999, 68.

6 R. M. Steers, Y. K. Shin, and G. R. Ungson, *The Chaebol: Korea's New Industrial Might*, New York: Ballinger, 1989, 66.

7 K. H. Chung, H. C. Lee, and K. H. Jung, *Korean Management: Global Strategy and Cultural Transformation*, Berlin: Walter de Gruyter, 1997, 146–7.

8 I. W. Jun, *The Strategic Management of Korean and Japanese Big Business Groups: A Comparison Study between Korean General Trading Companies and Japanese Sogo Shoshas*, doctoral thesis, Department of Management, University of Birmingham, 2009, 68. Available online: http://etheses.bham.ac.uk/258/ (accessed 4 November 2011).

9 Chung, Lee, and Jung, *Korean Management*, 151.

10 W.-S. Shim and R. M. Steers, "The Entrepreneurial Basis of Korean Enterprise: Past Accomplishments and Future Challenges," *Asia Pacific Business Review*, 2001, 7(4): 27.

11 Y.-H. Cho and J. Yoon, "The Origin and Function of Dynamic Collectivism: An Analysis of Korean Corporate Culture," *Asia Pacific Business Review*, 2001, 7(4): 80–1.

12 Samsung Electronics, *40 Years of Samsung Electronics*, 25.

13 L. Kim, *Imitation to Innovation: The Dynamics of Korea's Technological Learning*, Boston: Harvard Business School Press, 1997, 158.

14 W.-S. Park and G.-C. Yu, "HRM in Korea: Transformation and New Patterns," in Z. Rhee and E. Chang (eds), *Korean Business and Management: the Reality and the Vision*, Elisabeth, NJ: Hollym, 2002, 373.

15 L. Kim, "Crisis Construction and Organizational Learning: Capability Building in Catching-up at Hyundai Motor," *Organization Science*, 1998, 9(4): 510–6.

16 L. Kim, "The Dynamics of Samsung's Technological Learning in Semiconductors," *California Management Review*, 1997, 39(3): 90–4.

17 A. Michell, *Samsung Electronics and the Struggle for Leadership in the Electronics Industry*, Singapore: Wiley, 2010, 153–4.

18 K. Whitehall, "Samsung Mobile Phones," Author palace. Available online: http://www.authorpalace.com/technology/cell-phones/samsung-mobile-phones.html (accessed 15 September 2011).

19 Economist, "South Korea's Industrial Giants: Return of the Overlord," 31 March 2010.

20 Hankook Kyungjae, "Short, Surprise, Shocking… Chairman Lee Kun-hee's '3S' has worked," 17 June 2011. Short, Surprise, Shocking... 이건희 회장 "3S" 통했다, 한국경제.

21 Steers, Shin, and Ungson, *The Chaebol*, 39.

22 S.-J. Chang, *Sony vs. Samsung: The Inside Story of the Electronics Giants' Battle for Global Supremacy*, Singapore: Wiley, 2008, 149, 161.

23 Cho and Yoon, "The Origin and Function of Dynamic Collectivism," 75–6.

24 S.-J. Chang, *Financial Crisis and Transformation of Korean Business Groups: The Rise and Fall of Chaebols*, Cambridge: Cambridge University Press, 2003, 63–70.

25 One such exception is POSCO, which was founded by the government and later on privatized as a stock market listed company with dispersed ownership. Cf. POSCO, Posco 3.0 Global Symphony: Posco Sustainability Report 2009, 14. Available online: http://www.posco.co.kr/homepage/docs/kor2/dn/sustain/customer/2009_SR_eng.pdf (accessed 16 November 2011).

26 Chang, *Financial Crisis and Transformation of Korean Business Groups*, 104.

27 C. S. Chang and N. J. Chang, *The Korean Management System: Cultural, Political and Economic Foundations*, Westport, CO: Quorum, 1994, 122.

28 I. Yang, "Jeong Exchange and Collective Leadership in Korean Organizations," *Asia Pacific Journal of Management*, 2006, 23(3): 286.

29 T. Morden and D. Bowles, "Management in South Korea: a Review," *Management Decision*, 1998, 36(5): 321.

30 Chang and Chang, *The Korean Management System*, 47.
31 Cho and Yoon, "The Origin and Function of Dynamic Collectivism," 80–1.

9 Recruiting, training, and rewarding Tiger employees

 1 LG Corporation, About LG: Vision, Management Principles. Available online: http://
    www.lg.co.kr/about/vision_pop.jsp?num=1 (accessed 17 November 2011). LG 주식
    회사, LG 소개: 비전, 경영이념. Author's translation.
 2 R. M. Steers, *Made in Korea, Chung Ju Yung and the Rise of Hyundai*, New York and
    London: Routledge, 1999, 140.
 3 K. H. Chung, H. C. Lee, and K. H. Jung, *Korean Management: Global Strategy and
    Cultural Transformation,* Berlin: Walter de Gruyter, 1997, 164.
 4 J. Yee, "The Social Networks of Koreans," *Korea Journal*, 2000, 40(1): 335–7.
 5 T. M. Begley and W.-L. Tan, "The Socio-Cultural Environment for Entrepreneurship,"
    Journal of International Business Studies, 2001, 32(3): 539.
 6 C. S. Chang, "Human Resource Management in Korea," in K. H. Chung and H. C. Lee
    (eds), *Korean Managerial Dynamics*, New York: Praeger, 1989, 198.
 7 H.-C. Lee, "Transformation of Employment Practices in Korean Businesses," *Interna-
    tional Studies of Management and Organization*, 1999, 28(4): 34.
 8 Chung, Lee, and Jung, *Korean Management,* 169.
 9 Lee, "Transformation of Employment Practices in Korean Businesses," 31.
10 Chang, "Human Resource Management in Korea," 198–9.
11 Chung, Lee, and Jung, *Korean Management,* 175.
12 Chung, Lee, and Jung, *Korean Management,* 173.
13 Chung, Lee, and Jung, *Korean Management,* 172.
14 E. S. Cho, *Human Resource Development: The Past, Present and Future of Korean
    Companies*, Seoul: Beomhan, 2007, 81. 조은상, 인재개발론: 한국기업의 과거, 현재
    및 미래, 서울: 범한.
15 Chung, Lee, and Jung, *Korean Management,* 171–2.
16 M. Chen, *Asian management systems: Chinese, Japanese and Korean Styles of
    Business*, London: Thomson, 2004, 184.
17 Chung, Lee, and Jung, *Korean Management,* 181.
18 G. Ungson, R. Steers and S.-H. Park, *Korean Enterprise: The Quest for Globalization*,
    Boston, MA: Harvard Business School Press, 1997, 201.
19 Chen, *Asian Management Systems*, 185.
20 Chung, Lee, and Jung, *Korean Management,* 189–90.
21 W.-S. Park and G.-C. Yu, "HRM in Korea: Transformation and New Patterns," in
    Z. Rhee and E. Chang (eds), *Korean Business and Management: the Reality and the
    Vision*, Elisabeth, NJ: Hollym, 2002, 368.
22 J. Bae and C. Rowley, "Changes and Continuities in South Korean HRM," *Asia Pacific
    Business Review*, 2003, 9(4): 87–8.
23 J. Bae and G.-C.Yu, "HRM Configurations in Korean Venture Firms: Resource
    Availability, Institutional Force and Strategic Choice Perspectives," *International
    Journal of Human Resource Management,* 2005, 16(9): 1774.
24 Hankook Kyungjae, "Entering Executive Ranks at Samsung in Less Than 20 Years,
    Many Executives in their Early Forties to Enter the Stage," 22 October 2010. 삼성,
    20년차 안돼도 임원...40대 초반 임원 대거 등장할 듯, 한국경제.
25 Y.-H. Cho and J. Yoon, "The Origin and Function of Dynamic Collectivism: An
    Analysis of Korean Corporate Culture," *Asia Pacific Business Review*, 2001,
    7(4): 84.
26 M. Hemmert, "Innovation Management of Japanese and Korean Firms: A Comparative
    Analysis," *Asia Pacific Business Review*, 2008, 14(3): 304.
27 D.-O. Chang and J.-H. Chae, "The Transformation of Korean Labour Relations Since
    1997," *Journal of Contemporary Asia*, 2004, 34(4): 436.

28 OECD, OECD Statistical Extracts: Average Annual Hours Actually Worked per Worker. Available online: http://stats.oecd.org/Index.aspx?DataSetCode=ANHRS (accessed 17 November 2011).

29 M. L. Clifford, *Troubled Tiger: Businessmen, Bureaucrats, and Generals in South Korea,* Armonk, NY: Sharpe, 1998, 24.

30 Clifford, *Troubled Tiger,* 18.

31 Clifford, *Troubled Tiger,* 26–7.

32 Death Tolls for the Major Wars and Atrocities of the Twentieth Century, Korean War (1950–53), 3,000,000. Available online: http://necrometrics.com/20c1m.htm#Ko (accessed 17 November 2011).

33 H. Lee, *Economic History of Korea*, 2nd ed., Seoul: Beobmunsa, 1999, 556. 이헌창, 한국경제통사, 서울:법문사.

34 C. S. Chang and N. J. Chang, *The Korean Management System: Cultural, Political, Economic Foundations*, Westport, CO: Quorum, 1994, 163.

35 R. M. Steers, Y. K. Shin, and G. R. Ungson, *The Chaebol: Korea's New Industrial Might*, New York: Ballinger, 1989, 95.

36 A. Amsden, *Asia's Next Giant: South Korea and Late Industrialization*, Oxford: Oxford University Press, 1989, 217–22.

37 C. W. Sorensen, "Success and Education in Korea," *Comparative Education Review*, 1994, 38(1): 19.

38 OECD, *Education at a Glance 2011: OECD Indicators*, Paris: OECD Publishing, 2011, 15, 334.

39 J. Bae and J. J. Lawler, "Organizational and HRM Strategies in Korea: Impact on Firm Performance in an Emerging Economy," *Academy of Management Journal*, 2000, 43(3): 511.

10 Tiger Management in the world

1 LG Corporation, *LG 60 Year History: Passion for Customers and Challenging the Future,* Seoul, LG Corporation, 2007, 367. Author's translation. LG 60년사: 고객에 대한 열정, 미래를 향한 도전, 서울: 주식회사 LG.

2 K. Roth and A. J. Morrison, "An Empirical Analysis of the Integration-Responsiveness Framework in Global Industries," *Journal of International Business Studies*, 1990, 21(4): 543–4.

3 J.-A. Song, "South Korean Bosses Strive for a Global View," Financial Times, 13 November 2008.

4 J. Gamble, J. Morris, and B. Wilkinson, "Japanese and Korean Multinationals: The Replication and Integration of Their National Business Systems in China," *Asian Business and Management*, 2003, 2(3): 361–2.

5 J. R. Lee and M. Shin, *International Business*, 3rd ed., Seoul: Hongmoonsa, 2008, 407. 이장로, 신만수, 국제경영, 제3판, 서울: 홍문사.

6 K. Lee and X. He, "The Capability of the Samsung Group in Project Execution and Vertical Integration: Created in Korea, Replicated in China," *Asian Business and Management*, 2009, 8(3): 292–5.

7 Hankook Kyungjae, "The Secret of Customization: Creative Organizations Cheer the Market," 14 October 2008. 차별화의 비밀. 상상력을 파는 조직은 시장을 미소짓게 한다. 한국경제.

8 J. R. Lee, *International Marketing*, 5th ed., Seoul: Muyeok Kyongyongsa, 2008, 213. 이장로, 국제마케팅, 제5판, 서울: 무역경영사.

9 Y. Wang, M. N. Nam, and C. -S. Suh, "Firm Internationalization and Subsidiary Roles: The Case of Hyundai Motor Company," paper presented at the 4th World Congress of Korean Studies, Seoul, 21–24 September 2008, 21.

10 J.-S. Imm, "Stark Difference between Japan and Korea in Investment Methods in India," *POSRI Chindia Quarterly*, 2011, 1(1): 91.

11 S. Kabiraj and J. Shanmugan, "Indigenous Customer Relationship Management Practices in Indian Automobile Companies: Strategic Implications," *International Journal of Management Perspectives*, 2009, 4(1): 13–6.

12 Y. Paik and Y. S. Park, "The Changing Face of Korean Management of Overseas Affiliates" in C. Rowley and Y. Paik (eds), *The Changing Face of Korean Management*, Oxon: Routledge, 2009, 165–70.

13 R. D. Lansbury, C.-S. Suh, and S.-H. Kwon, *The Global Korean Motor Industry: The Hyundai Motor Company's global strategy*, Oxon: Routledge, 2007, 99.

14 Hankook Kyungjae, "Overtime Work and Extra Shifts OK with Chinese Workers: Hynix's Koreanization Strategy Worked," 22 November 2010. 中직원 "잔업, 특근도 OK"... 하이닉스 '한국화 전략' 통했다, 한국경제.

15 J.-S. Imm, "Stark Difference between Japan and Korea in Investment Methods in India," 90–1.

16 For a detailed discussion of the differences between national cultures and their implications for work organization and management, see G. Hofstede, *Culture's Consequences: Comparing Values, Behaviors, Institutions and Organizations across Nations*, 2nd ed., Thousand Oaks, CA: Sage, 2001.

17 Paik and Park, "The Changing Face of Korean Management of Overseas Affiliates," 177–8.

18 Lansbury, Suh, and Kwon, *The Global Korean Motor Industry*, 108.

19 Lansbury, Suh, and Kwon, *The Global Korean Motor Industry*, 92–3.

20 Paik and Park, "The Changing Face of Korean Management of Overseas Affiliates," 178–9.

21 Paik and Park, "The Changing Face of Korean Management of Overseas Affiliates," 172–6.

22 For instance, in a recently administered survey among Korean expatriate managers dispatched to the US, respondents reported an average local living experience of one and a half years before they assumed their current work assignment. K. Kim and J. W. Slocum, "Individual Differences and Expatriate Assignment Effectiveness: The Case of U.S.-based Korean Expatriates," *Journal of World Business*, 2008, 43(1): 116.

23 Paik and Park, "The Changing Face of Korean Management of Overseas Affiliates," 171–6.

24 Lee and Shin, *International Business*, 7.

25 K. J. Freeze and K.-W. Chung, *Design Strategy at Samsung Electronics: Becoming a Top-Tier Company,* Case Study DMI021, Boston, MA: Harvard Business School Publishing, 2008, 17.

26 Author's interview, June 2011.

27 Hankook Kyungjae, "The Anchor of 'Global Lotte' has been Pulled: Building more than 10 Lotte Towns in China, Russia, Vietnam and Indonesia," 31 October 2010. "글로벌 롯데" 닻 올렸다: 中, 러, 베트남, 인도네시아에 "롯데타운" 10개 이상 만든다, 한국경제.

28 Wang, Nam, and Suh, "Firm Internationalization and Subsidiary Roles," 18–22.

29 K.-T. Kim, S.-K. Rhee, and J. Oh, "The Strategic Role Evolution of Foreign Automotive Parts Subsidiaries in China," *International Journal of Operations and Production Management,* 2011, 31(1): 40–5.

30 Author's interview, June 2011.

31 One recent case for this new approach is SK Group. Hankook Kyungjae, "Headquarters where the Markets are: SK builds a New Base for its Global Operations," 22 February 2010. 시장 있는 곳에 "헤드쿼터"... SK, 글로벌사업 새판 짠다, 한국경제.

32 S.-J. Chang, *Sony vs. Samsung: The Inside Story of the Electronics Giants' Battle for Global Supremacy*, Singapore: Wiley, 2008, 94–8.

33 Paik and Park, "The Changing Face of Korean Management of Overseas Affiliates," 169–70.

34 Well known examples of such "traveling executives" are Daewoo's former chairman, Kim Woo-choong, and the current SK chairman, Chey Taewon. Hankook Kyungjae,

"The Chairman Commuting to China: On 1 July We Will Write New SK history," 19 April 2010. 중국으로 "출근" 하는 회장님... "7월1일은 SK 새 역사 쓰는날, 한국경제.

11 Dynamic Korea

1 G.-C. Yu and C. Rowley, "The Changing Face of Korean Human Resource Management" in C. Rowley and Y. Paik (eds), *The Changing Face of Korean Management*, Oxon: Routledge, 2009, 45.
2 R. Baldwin and D. Taglioni, "The Great Trade Collapse and Trade Imbalances" in Centre for Economic Policy Research (ed.), *The Great Trade Collapse: Causes, Consequences and Prospects*, London: Centre for Economic Policy Research, 2009, 48.
3 E. M. Kim, *Big Business, Strong State: Collusion and Conflict in South Korean Development, 1960–1990*, Albany, NY: State University of New York Press, 1997, 226.
4 D. Kirk, "South Korea to Open Inquiry Into 6 Large Conglomerates," New York Times, 5 March 2003.
5 YTN News, "Job Generation through Co-prosperity is Social Policy, says President Lee Myung-bak," 14 September 2010. 이명박 대통령 "동반성장 통한 일자리 창출이 서민 정책", YTN 뉴스.
6 Kim, *Big Business, Strong State*, 204.
7 O. Y. Kwon, *International Business in Korea: The Evolution of the Market in the Globalization Era*, Cheltenham: Edward Elgar, 2008, 210.
8 S. J. Cho, "A 20 Year Review of Industrial Relations through Organizational and Industrial Dispute Statistics," *Monthly Labor Review*, No. 30, June 2007: 19. 조성재, "조직과 분규 통계로 본 노사관계 20년", 월간 노동리뷰 30호.
9 R. M. Steers, *Made in Korea: Chung Ju Yung and the Rise of Hyundai*, New York: Routledge, 1999, 147–8.
10 Kwon, *International Business in Korea*, 210.
11 The labor participation rate of Korean working age women increased from 38.6 percent in 1963 to 46.1 percent in 1980, 51.2 percent in 1990, 55.8 percent in 2000, and 59.0 percent in 2008. OECD, Labour Force Statistics, Summary Tables. Available online: http://stats.oecd.org/BrandedView.aspx?oecd_bv_id=lfs-data-en&doi=lfs-lfs-data-en (accessed 18 November 2011).
12 N. Kim and C. Rowley, "The Changing Face of Korean Women in Management," in C. Rowley and Y. Paik (eds), *The Changing Face of Korean Management*, Oxon: Routledge, 2009, 200–1.
13 According to the most recent education statistics published by the Ministry of Education, Science and Technology, 47.3 percent of all college students and 48.6 percent of all graduates from master programs in 2010 were female. Ministry of Education, Science and Technology, Statistics Service. Available online: http://std.kedi.re.kr/index.jsp (accessed 18 November 2011).
14 Kim and Rowley, "The Changing Face of Korean Women in Management," 196.
15 Kim and Rowley, "The Changing Face of Korean Women in Management," 209.
16 O. Y. Kwon, *The Korean Economy in Transition: An Institutional Perspective*, Cheltenham: Edward Elgar, 2010, 320.
17 T. Hussain, *Diamond Dilemma: Shaping Korea for the 21st Century*, Seoul, 2006, 139.
18 G.-S. Park and A. E. Kim, "Changes in Attitude toward Work and Workers' Identity in Korea," *Korea Journal*, 2005, 45(3): 48.
19 J. H.-J. Choi, "The City of Connections: Urban Social Networking in Seoul," Proceedings MindTrek: *12th international conference on entertainment and media in a ubiquitous era*, Tampere, Finland, 2008, 190–1.
20 P. R. J. Trim and Y.-I. Lee, "Insights from Teaching Japanese and Korean Students using Group Work and Case Studies" in D. Saunders and N. Smalley (eds), *The International Gaming and Simulation Research Yearbook*, London: Kogan Page, 2000, 121.

21 Author's interview, August 2011.
22 S. Cho and T. Youn, "Changes in Corporate Governance of Korean Enterprises after the Financial Crisis" in D. Kang (ed.), *Government Policies and Corporate Strategies under Structural Changes and Dynamism: The Cases of Korea and China*, Seoul: Korea Development Institute, 2008, 28.
23 W. Kang, "The Changing Face of Korean Finance Management" in C. Rowley and Y. Paik (eds), *The Changing Face of Korean Management*, Oxon: Routledge, 2009, 114–5.
24 D. Southerton, "Samsung Group Court Ruling Upheld," Korea Legal.org, 31 May 2009. Available online: http://www.koreaexpertwitness.com/blog/uncategorized/120/ (accessed 18 November 2011).
25 Kwon, *International Business in Korea*, 195.
26 D. -W. Kim, "Personal and Managerial Capitalism: Evidence from Management in the Korean Chaebol," paper presented at the 14th International Economic History Congress, 21–25 August 2006, Helsinki, Finland, 17.
27 A. Michell, *Samsung Electronics and the Struggle for Leadership of the Electronics Industry*, Singapore: Wiley, 2010, 5–7.
28 LG Corporation, About LG: Vision, Management Principles. Available online: http://www.lg.co.kr/about/vision_pop.jsp?num=1 (accessed 17 November 2011). LG 주식회사, LG 소개: 비전, 경영이념.
29 Samsung Electronics, Samsung Integrity Management. Available online: http://www.samsung.com/sec/aboutsamsung/Sustainability/integritymanagement.html (accessed 18 November 2011). 삼성전자, Samsung 정도경영.
30 Kwon, *The Korean Economy in Transition*, 236.
31 Hankook Kyungjae, "This is Co-prosperity: When Korean Final Car Producers Came Out Well, Core Suppliers also Achieved 10-fold Growth in 10 Years," 25 April 2011. 이것이 동반성장: 한국 완성차업체 잘 나가니 핵심 부품업체도 "10 10질주", 한국경제.
32 J. Kim and M. Hemmert, "Trust Formation by Suppliers in the Korean Manufacturing Sector," paper presented at the 28th EAMSA Conference, Gothenburg, Sweden, 23–26 November 2011, 29.
33 Forum of Co-prosperity of Large Firms and SMEs, Seoul, 26 October 2010, attached materials. 대 중소기업 동반성장 포럼, 서울, 부록.
34 Kwon, *International Business in Korea*, 210–2.
35 Kwon, *The Korean Economy in Transition,* 317.
36 Hankook Kyungjae, "The First Great Compromise between Unions, Companies, Government and Civic Groups in Five Years: Unions Accept Pay Cuts, Companies Keep Employment, the Government Extends the Social Security Net." 24 February 2009. 노사민정 5년만의 대타협 勞 임금절감 – 使 고용유지 – 政 사회안전망 확충. 한국경제.
37 S. J. Cho, "A 20 Year Review of Industrial Relations through Organizational and Industrial Dispute Statistics," *Monthly Labor Review*, No. 30, June 2007: 21. 조성재, "조직과 분규 통계로 본 노사관계 20년", 월간 노동리뷰 30호.
38 G.-C. Yu and C. Rowley, "The Changing Face of Korean Human Resource Management" in C. Rowley and Y. Paik (eds), *The Changing Face of Korean Management*, Oxon: Routledge, 2009, 35.
39 Y.-I. Lee, "South Korean Companies in Transition: an Evolving Strategic Management Style," *Strategic Change*, 2004, 13(1): 31.
40 Kwon, *International Business in Korea*, 221.
41 L. Jung, "National Labour Law Profile: Republic of Korea (South Korea), Dialogue, Industrial Employment Relations Department, International Labour Organization." Available online: http://www.ilo.org/public/english/dial ogue/ifpdial/info/national/kor.htm#pl (accessed 18 November 2011).
42 Author's interview, July 2011.
43 E.-S. Lee and S. Kim, "Best Practices and Performance-Based HR System in Korea," *Seoul Journal of Business*, 2006, 12(1): 9.

44 Ministry of Employment and Labor, MOEL Survey Data, Survey on Labor Conditions by Type of Employment, various years. Available online: http://www.moel.go.kr/english/statistics/MOL_Survey_Data.jsp (accessed 18 November 2011).
45 J. Lee and C. Rowley, "The Changing Face of Women Managers in South Korea" in C. Rowley and V. Yukongdi (eds), *The Changing Face of Women Managers in Asia*, Oxon: Routledge, 2009, 154.
46 Kim and Rowley, "The Changing Face of Korean Women in Management." 204–7.
47 Author's interview, August 2011.
48 Author's interview, September 2011.
49 Author's interviews, July 2011.
50 Hussain, *Diamond Dilemma*, 138–9.
51 J. R. Renshaw, *Korean Women Managers and Corporate Culture: Changing Tradition, Choosing Empowerment, Creating Change*, Oxon: Routledge, 2011, 87.
52 A. Michell, *Samsung Electronics and the Struggle for Leadership of the Electronics Industry*, 190–1.

12 Studying Tiger Management

1 V. Kotelnikov, "25 Lessons from Jack Welch: Management Insight and Leadership Secrets of the Legendary Former CEO of GE." Available online: http://www.1000ventures.com/business_guide/mgmt_new-model_25lessons-welch.html (accessed 3 November 2011).
2 J. P. MacDuffie and F. K. Pil, "Changes in Auto Industry Employment Practices: An International Overview" in T. A. Kochan, R. D. Lansbury, and J. P. MacDuffie (eds), *After Lean Production: Evolving Employment Practices in the World Auto Industry*, Ithaca, NY: Cornell University Press, 1997, 26–32.
3 A. Inkpen, "Knowledge Transfer and International Joint Ventures: the Case of NUMMI and General Motors," *Strategic Management Journal*, 2008, 29(4): 452.
4 A. K. Gupta and V. Govindarajan, "Knowledge Flows Within Multinational Corporations," *Strategic Management Journal*, 2000, 21(4): 475–6.
5 M. Javidan, G. K. Stahl, F. Brodbeck, and C. P. M. Wilderom, "Cross-border Transfer of Knowledge: Cultural Lessons from Project GLOBE," *Academy of Management Executive*, 2005, 19(2): 64–71.
6 Economist, "Asia's New Model Company," 1 October 2011.
7 Y. Fukagawa, "What gives Korean Companies their Edge?", *Japan Echo Web*, No. 3, October–November 2010, 9–10. Available online: http://www.japanechoweb.jp/wp-content/uploads/downloads/2010/11/jew0312.pdf (accessed 1 November 2011).
8 T. Hussain, *Diamond Dilemma: Shaping Korea for the 21st Century*, Seoul, 2006, 103–7.
9 See, for example, J. P. Womack, D. T. Jones, and D. Roos, *The Machine that Changed the World*, Rawson Associates: New York, 1990, and K. B. Clark and T. Fujimoto, *Product Development Performance: Strategy, Organization, and Management in the World Auto Industry*, Boston: Harvard Business School Press, 1991.
10 M. Holweg, "The Genealogy of Lean Production," *Journal of Operations Management*, 2007, 25(2): 425–8.
11 Javidan, Stahl, Brodbeck, and Wilderom, "Cross-border Transfer of Knowledge," 71–4.

Bibliography

Abegglen, J. C. and G. Stalk, *Kaisha: The Japanese Corporation*, New York: Basic Books, 1985.

Ahnlab, About Ahnlab: Overview. Available online: http://www.ahnlab.com/company/site/eng/about/ overview.jsp (accessed 12 November 2011).

—— About AhnLab: Introduction of Founder. Available online: http://www.ahnlab.com/company/site/about/founder_retire.jsp (accessed 13 November 2011). About AhnLab: 설립자소개.

Allen, A.-L. and J. Holt, *Exploring North-East Asia: China, Japan, Korea*, Carlton: Curriculum, 1999.

Amsden, A., *Asia's Next Giant: South Korea and Late Industrialization*, New York and Oxford: Oxford University Press, 1989.

Bae, J. and J. J. Lawler, "Organizational and HRM Strategies in Korea: Impact on Firm Performance in an Emerging Economy," *Academy of Management Journal*, 2000, 43(3): 502–17.

Bae, J. and C. Rowley, "Changes and Continuities in South Korean HRM," *Asia Pacific Business Review*, 2003, 9(4): 76–105.

Bae, J. and G.-C.Yu, "HRM Configurations in Korean Venture Firms: Resource Availability, Institutional Force and Strategic Choice Perspectives," *International Journal of Human Resource Management*, 2005, 16(9): 1759–82.

Baldwin, R. and D. Taglioni, "The Great Trade Collapse and Trade Imbalances" in *The Great Trade Collapse: Causes, Consequences and Prospects*, London: Centre for Economic Policy Research, 2009, 47–56.

Bank of Korea, *Financial Statement Analysis for 2009*, Seoul: Bank of Korea, 2010.

—— Economic Statistics System. Available online: http://ecos.bok.or.kr/EIndex_en.jsp (accessed 7 November 2011).

Begley, T. M. and W.-L. Tan, "The Socio-Cultural Environment for Entrepreneurship," *Journal of International Business Studies*, 2001, 32(3): 537–53.

Chacksfield, M., "Samsung Becomes the World's Biggest Technology Company. HP Drops to Second Place," World of Tech News, 29 January 2010. Available online: http://www.techradar.com/news/world-of-tech/samsung-becomes-the-world-s-biggest-technology-company-667152 (accessed 13 November 2011).

Chang, C. S., "Human Resource Management in Korea" in K. H. Chung and H. C. Lee (eds), *Korean Managerial Dynamics*, New York: Praeger, 1989, 195–205.

Chang, C. S. and N. J. Chang, *The Korean Management System: Cultural, Political, Economic Foundations,* Westport, CN: Quorum, 1994.

Chang, D.-O and J.-H. Chae, "The Transformation of Korean Labour Relations Since 1997," *Journal of Contemporary Asia,* 2004, 34(4): 427–48.

Chang, S.-J., *Financial Crisis and Transformation of Korean Business Groups: The Rise and Fall of Chaebols,* Cambridge: Cambridge University Press, 2003.

—— "Business Groups in East Asia: Post-crisis Restructuring and New Growth," *Asia Pacific Journal of Management,* 2006, 23(4): 407–17.

—— *Sony vs. Samsung: The Inside Story of the Electronics Giants' Battle for Global Supremacy,* Singapore: Wiley, 2008.

Chen, M., *Asian Management Systems: Chinese, Japanese and Korean Styles of Business,* London: Thomson, 2004.

Chen, M.-J., *Inside Chinese Business: A Guide for Managers Worldwide,* Boston: Harvard Business School Press, 2001.

Cho, D.-S., *Research on Korean Business Groups,* rev. ed., Seoul: Maeil Kyungjae Sinmunsa, 1991. 조동성, 한국재벌연구, 개정1판, 서울: 매일경제신문사.

—— "From Subsidizer to Regulator – The Changing Role of Korean Government," *Long Range Planning,* 1992, 25(6): 48–55.

Cho, E. S., *Human Resource Development: The Past, Present and Future of Korean Companies,* Seoul: Beomhan, 2007. 조은상, 인재개발론: 한국기업의 과거, 현재 및 미래, 서울: 범한.

Cho, S. J., "A 20 Year Review of Industrial Relations through Organizational and Industrial Dispute Statistics," *Monthly Labor Review,* No. 30, June 2007, 3–29. 조성재, "조직과 분규 통계로 본 노사관계 20년", 월간 노동리뷰 30호.

Cho, Y.-H. and J. Yoon, "The Origin and Function of Dynamic Collectivism: An Analysis of Korean Corporate Culture," *Asia Pacific Business Review,* 2001, 7(4): 70–88.

Cho, S. and T. Youn, "Changes in Corporate Governance of Korean Enterprises after the Financial Crisis" in D. Kang (ed.), *Government Policies and Corporate Strategies under Structural Changes and Dynamism: The Cases of Korea and China,* Seoul: Korea Development Institute, 2008, 15–38.

Choe, S. and C. Pattnaik, "The Transformation of Korean Business Groups after the Asian Crisis," *Journal of Contemporary Asia,* 2007, 37(2): 232–55.

Choe, S. and T. Roehl, "What to Shed and What to Keep: Corporate Transformation in Korean Business Groups," *Long Range Planning,* 2007, 40(4–5): 465–87.

Choi, C. and C. Lee, *Managerial Values and Human Resource Management at Korea's Large Business Groups,* Paju: Hankook Haksul Jeongbo, 2005. 최종태, 이준우, 한국 대기업집단 경영가치와 인적자원관리, 파주: 한국학술정보.

Choi, J. H.-J., "The City of Connections: Urban Social Networking in Seoul," Proceedings MindTrek: 12th International Conference on Entertainment and Media in a Ubiquitous Era, Tampere, Finland, 2008, 189–93.

Chon, S. H., S. O. Park, S. M. Oh, and J. S. Park, *Outsourcing Strategy of Reigncom, the MP3 Corporation,* KAIST Case Competition, Seoul, 2004.

Chosun Ilbo, "Adding One Subsidiary Every Three Days... Half of the 'Octopus Legs' Lose Money," 22 June 2011. "사흘에 하나씩 계열사 늘려... '문어발의 성적' 절반이 적자", 조선일보.

—— "Hyundai Kia, after China, India, and Europe, now also Overtaking Japanese in South America, only North America Remaining," July 4, 2011. 현대 기아, 中, 印, 유럽 이어 南美서 日추월, 北美만남아, 조선일보.

Chung, K. H., H. C. Lee, and J. H. Jung, *Korean Management: Global Strategy and Cultural Transformation*, Berlin: Walter de Gruyter, 1997.

Chung, Y.-I., "Chaebol Entrepreneurs in the Early Stage of Korean Economic Development," *Journal of Modern Korean Studies*, 1985, 2 (Dec): 15–28.

Clark, K. B. and T. Fujimoto, *Product Development Performance: Strategy, Organization, and Management in the World Auto Industry*, Boston: Harvard Business School Press, 1991.

Clifford, M. L., *Troubled Tiger: Businessmen, Bureaucrats, and Generals in South Korea*, 2nd ed., Armond: Sharpe, 1998.

CNN Money, Fortune Global 500: Our Annual Ranking of the World's Largest Corporations. Available online: http://money.cnn.com/magazines/fortune/global500/2011/ (accessed 3 December 2011).

Daewoo Global Management Research Study Group, *30 Year History of Daewoo*, Seoul: Daewoo Global Management Research Study Group, 2010. 대우세계경영연구회, 대우 30년사, 서울: 대우세계경영연구회.

Death Tolls for the Major Wars and Atrocities of the Twentieth Century, Korean War (1950–53): 3,000,000. Available online: http://necrometrics.com/20c1m.htm#Ko (accessed 17 November 2011).

Dorfman, P. W., J. P. Howell, S. Hibino, J. K. Lee, U. Tate, and A. Bautista, "Leadership in Western and Asian Countries: Commonalities and Differences in Effective Leadership Processes Across Cultures," *Leadership Quarterly*, 1997, 8(3): 233–74.

Eckert, C. J., *Offspring of Empire: The Koch'ang Kims and the Colonial Origins of Korean Capitalism 1876–1945*, Seattle and London: University of Washington Press, 1991.

Economist, "South Korea's Pop-cultural Exports: Hallyu, Yeah! A 'Korean Wave' Washes Warmly over Asia," 25 January 2010.

—— "South Korea's Industrial Giants: Return of the Overlord," 31 March 2010.

—— "Asia's New Model Company," 1 October 2011.

Euh, Y.-D. and J. H. Rhee, "Lessons from the Korean Crisis: Policy and Managerial Implications," *Long Range Planning*, 2007, 40(4/5): 431–45.

Forum of Co-prosperity of Large Firms and SMEs, Seoul, 26 October 2010, attached materials. 대 중소기업 동반성장 포럼, 서울, 부록.

Francks, P., *Japanese Economic Development*, 2nd ed., London: Routledge, 1999.

Freeze, K. J. and K.-W. Chung, *Design Strategy at Samsung Electronics: Becoming a Top-Tier Company.* Case Study DMI021, Boston, MA: Harvard Business School Publishing, 2008.

—— *Epilogue March 2008: What Actually Happened at Samsung Design*, Case Study DMI023. Boston, MA: Harvard Business School Publishing, 2008.

Fukagawa, Y., "What gives Korean Companies their Edge?", *Japan Echo Web*, No. 3, October–November 2010: 9–10. Available online: http://www.japanechoweb.jp/wp-content/uploads/downloads/2010/11/jew0312.pdf (accessed 1 November 2011).

Gamble, J., J. Morris, and B. Wilkinson, "Japanese and Korean Multinationals: The Replication and Integration of Their National Business Systems in China," *Asian Business and Management*, 2003, 2(3): 347–69.

Gartner, Gartner Newsroom, "Gartner Says 428 Million Mobile Communication Devices Sold Worldwide in First Quarter 2011, a 19 Percent Increase Year-on-Year." Press Release, 19 May 2011. Available online: http://www.gartner.com/it/page.jsp?id=1689814 (accessed 10 November 2011).

Gupta, A. K. and V. Govindarajan, "Knowledge Flows within Multinational Corporations," *Strategic Management Journal*, 2000, 21(4): 473–96.

Hankook Kyungjae, "LG Electronics Overseas Campaign: Now Africa," 20 June 2008. LG전자 해외공략 "이젠 아프리카다", 한국경제.

—— "The Secret of Customization: Creative Organizations Cheer the Market," 14 October 2008. 차별화의 비밀. 상상력을 파는 조직은 시장을 미소짓게 한다. 한국경제.

—— "The First Great Compromise between Unions, Companies, Government and Civic Groups in Five Years: Unions Accept Pay Cuts, Companies keep Employment, the Government Extends the Social Security Net," 24 February 2009. 노사민정 5년만의 대타협 勞 임금절감 – 使 고용유지 – 政 사회안전망 확충. 한국경제.

—— "Hyundai Motor Shows Next Generation Hybrid for the First Time in Germany," 14 September 2009. "현대차, 차세대 하이브리드 독서 첫공개", 한국경제.

—— "Headquarters Where the Markets Are: SK Builds a New Base for its Global Operations," 23 February 2010. 시장 있는 곳에 "헤드쿼터"... SK, 글로벌사업 새판 짠다, 한국경제.

—— "LG Electronics Says Solar Batteries Will Grow TV and Cellular Phone Business in 10 Years," 11 March 2010. "LG 전자 "태양전지, 10년후 TV, 휴대폰만큼 커진다," 한국경제.

—— "The Chairman Commuting to China: On July 1st We Will Write New SK history," 19 April 2010. 중국으로 "출근" 하는 회장님... "7월1일은 SK 새역사 쓰는날, 한국경제.

—— "Entering Executive Ranks at Samsung in Less Than 20 Years, Many Executives in Their Early Forties to Enter the Stage," 22 October 2010. 삼성, 20년차 안돼도 임원...40대 초반 임원 대거 등장할 듯, 한국경제.

—— "The Anchor of 'Global Lotte' Has Been Pulled: Building More Than 10 Lotte Towns in China, Russia, Vietnam and Indonesia," 31 October 2010. "글로벌 롯데" 닻 올렸다: 中, 러, 배트남, 인도네시아에 "롯데타운" 10개 이상 만든다, 한국경제.

—— "Overtime Work and Extra Shifts OK with Chinese Workers: Hynix's Koreanization Strategy Worked," 22 November 2010. 中직원 "잔업, 특근도 OK"... 하이닉스 "한국화 전략" 통했다, 한국경제.

—— "This is Co-prosperity: When Korean Final Car Producers Came Out Well, Core Suppliers also Achieved 10-fold Growth in 10 years," 25 April 2011. 이것이 동반성장: 한국완 성차업체 잘 나가니 핵심 부품업체도 "10 10질주", 한국경제.

—— "Hyundai Kia Motor Breaking for the First Time Through 10% Market Share in US Market," 7 June 2011. 현대 기아차, 美 시장 점유율 첫 10% 돌파, 한국경제.

—— "Short, Surprise, Shocking... Chairman Lee Kun-hee's '3S' has Worked," 17 June 2011. Short, Surprise, Shocking... 이건희 회장 "3S" 통했다, 한국경제.

Hanwha Group, Overview. Available online: http://www.hanwha.co.kr/english/index.jsp (accessed 15 November 2011).

Hassink, R. and D.-H. Shin, "South Korea's Shipbuilding Industry: From a Couple of Cathedrals in the Desert to an Innovative Cluster," *Asian Journal of Technology Innovation*, 2005, 13(2): 133–55.

Hemmert, M., "Innovation Management of Japanese and Korean Firms: A Comparative Analysis," *Asia Pacific Business Review*, 2008, 14(3): 293–314.

Hobday, M., *Innovation in East Asia: The Challenge to Japan*. Cheltenham: Edward Elgar, 1995.

Hofstede, G., *Culture's Consequences*, 2nd ed., Thousand Oaks: Sage, 2001.

Holweg, M. "The Genealogy of Lean Production," *Journal of Operations Management*, 2007, 25(2): 420–37.

Humax, Milestones. Available online: http://www.humaxdigital.com/global/abouthumax/milestones.asp (accessed 13 November 2011).

Hur, C., "Culture, Goal-Oriented Communication (Leadership), and a Fast Growing Organization: the Case of Samsung Electronics," mimeo. Available online: http://www.ad.co.kr/lit/report/download.xhr?objectType=LR&objectUkey=3423&fileName=3423.pdf (accessed 7 November 2011).

Hussain, T., *Diamond Dilemma: Shaping Korea for the 21st Century*, Seoul, 2006.

IFI Claims Patent Services, IFI Claims Announces Top Global Companies Ranked By 2010 US Patents. Available online: http://www.ificlaims.com/news/top-patents.html (accessed 13 November 2011).

IISI – World Steel Association, World Steel Top Producers 2010. Available online: http://www.worldsteel.org/statistics/top-producers.html (accessed 7 November 2011).

Imm, J.-S., "Stark Difference Between Japan and Korea in Investment Methods in India," *POSRI Chindia Quarterly*, 2011, 1(1): 85–91.

Inkpen, A. "Knowledge Transfer and International Joint Ventures: the Case of NUMMI and General Motors," *Strategic Management Journal*, 2008, 29(4): 447–53.

Inkpen, A. and K. Ramaswamy, "End of the Multinational: Emerging Markets Redraw the Picture," *Journal of Business Strategy*, 2007, 28(5): 4–12.

Interbrand, Best Global Brands 2010. Available online: http://www.interbrand.com/ko/best-global-brands/best-global-brands-2008/best-global-brands-2010.aspx (accessed 13 November 2011).

iSuppli, Market Watch. Available online: http://www.isuppli.com/marketwatch/Pages/Default.aspx (accessed 3 December 2011).

Iwasaki, Y., "Wither Thailand?" in W. C. Hunter, G. G. Kaufman, and T. H. Krueger (eds), *The Asian Financial Crisis: Origins, Implications, and Solutions*, Boston: Kluwer, 1999, 193–200.

Javidan, M., G. K. Stahl, F. Brodbeck, and C. P. M. Wilderom, "Cross-border transfer of knowledge: Cultural lessons from Project GLOBE," *Academy of Management Executive*, 2005, 19(2): 59–76.

Jin, H.-J., "Lee Byung-chull: the Man who Founded the Samsung Empire," Korea Herald, 30 March 2010.

Jo, H. J. and J.-S. You, "Transferring Production Systems: An Institutionalist Account of Hyundai Motor Company in the United States," *Journal of East Asian Studies*, 2011, (11): 41–73.

Juhn, D. S., "The Development of Korean Entrepreneurship" in A. C. Nahm (ed.), *Korea Under Japanese Colonial Rule*, Center for Korean Studies, Western Michigan University, 1973, 113–34.

Jun, I. W., *The Strategic Management of Korean and Japanese Big Business Groups: A Comparison Study between Korean General Trading Companies and Japanese Sogo Shoshas*, doctoral thesis, Department of Management, University of Birmingham, 2009. Available online: http://etheses.bham.ac.uk/258/ (accessed 4 November 2011).

Jung, L., "National Labour Law Profile: Republic of Korea (South Korea), Dialogue, Industrial Employment Relations Department, International Labour Organization." Available online: http://www.ilo.org/public/english/dial ogue/ifpdial/info/national/kor.htm#pl (accessed 18 November 2011).

Jwa, S.-H. and I. K. Lee, "Introduction" in *Korean Chaebol in Transition: Road Ahead and Agenda*, Seoul: Korea Economic Research Institute, 2000, 17–34.

Kabiraj, S. and J. Shanmugan, "Indigenous Customer Relationship Management Practices in Indian Automobile Companies: Strategic Implications," *International Journal of Management Perspectives*, 2009, 4(1): 1–25.

Kang, C. W., "An Analysis of Japanese Policy and Economic Change in Korea" in A. C. Nahm (ed.), *Korea Under Japanese Colonial Rule*, Center for Korean Studies, Western Michigan University, 1973, 77–88.

Kang, W., "The Changing Face of Korean Finance Management" in C. Rowley and Y. Paik (eds), *The Changing Face of Korean Management*, Oxon: Routledge, 2009, 100–25.

KBS World, "Hyundai Kia Overseas Production to Top 50% Next Year," 11 November 2010. Available online: http://world.kbs.co.kr/english/news/news_Ec_detail.htm?No=77104 (accessed 13 November 2011).

Kim, C. J., *The History of Korea*, Westport, CT: Greenwood Press, 2005.

Kim, D.-J., "Falls from Grace and Lessons from Failure: Daewoo and Medison," *Long Range Planning*, 2007, 40(4/5): 446–64.

Kim, D.-W., "Personal and Managerial Capitalism: Evidence from Management in the Korean Chaebol," paper presented at the 14th International Economic History Congress, 21–25 August 2006, Helsinki, Finland.

Kim, E. M., *Big Business, Strong State: Collusion and Conflict in South Korean Development, 1960–1990*, Albany: State University of New York Press, 1997.

—— *The Four Asian Tigers: Economic Development and the Global Political Economy*, San Diego: Academic Press, 1998.

Kim, H., R. E. Hoskisson, L. Tihanyi, and J. Hong, "The Evolution of Diversified Business Groups in Emerging Markets: the Lessons from Chaebols in Korea," *Asia Pacific Journal of Management*, 2004, 21(1): 25–48.

Kim, I. K., "Confucian Culture and Economic Development: Focusing on Korea and Japan," *Hanil Kyeongsang Nonsip*, 1984, 1 (0): 1–24. 김일곤, 유교문화권 (儒敎文化圈)의 경제발전(經濟發展) –한국(韓國)과 일본(日本)을 중심(中心)으로-, 한일경상논집.

Kim, J. and M. Hemmert, "Trust Formation by Suppliers in the Korean Manufacturing Sector," paper presented at the 28th EAMSA Conference, Gothenburg, Sweden, 23–26 November 2011.

Kim, K.-T., S.-K. Rhee, and J. Oh, "The Strategic Role Evolution of Foreign Automotive Parts Subsidiaries in China," *International Journal of Operations and Production Management*, 2011, 31(1): 31–55.

Kim, K. and J. W. Slocum, "Individual Differences and Expatriate Assignment Effectiveness: The Case of U.S.-based Korean Expatriates," *Journal of World Business*, 2008, 43(1): 109–26.

Kim, L., *Imitation to Innovation: The Dynamics of Korea's Technological Learning*, Boston: Harvard Business School Press, 1997.

—— "The Dynamics of Samsung's Technological Learning in Semiconductors," *California Management Review*, 1997, 39(3): 86–100.

—— "Crisis Construction and Organizational Learning: Capability Building in Catching-up at Hyundai Motor," *Organization Science*, 1998, 9(4): 506–21.

Kim, N. and C. Rowley, "The Changing Face of Korean Women in Management" in C. Rowley and Y. Paik (eds), *The Changing Face of Korean Management*, Oxon: Routledge, 2009, 189–214.

Kirk, D., *Korean Dynasty: Hyundai and Chung Ju Yung*, Armonk, NY: Sharpe, 1994.

—— "South Korea to Open Inquiry Into 6 Large Conglomerates," New York Times, 5 March 2003.

Korea Fair Trade Commission, *Companies Affiliated with Large Business Groups*, Seoul: Korea Fair Trade commission, various years. 공정거래위원회, 대규모 기업집단 소속회사 현황, 서울: 공정거래위원회.

Korea IT Times, "30 Korean Software Companies Worthy of Global Recognition in 2012," 15 July 2011.

—— "AhnLab Considers Overseas M&A," 22 October 2009.

Korea Times, "Venture firm Humax Finally Thriving," 31 January 2011.

Kotelnikov, V., "25 Lessons from Jack Welch: Management Insight and Leadership Secrets of the Legendary Former CEO of GE." Available online: http://www.1000ventures. com/business_guide/mgmt_new-model_25lessons-welch.html (accessed 3 November 2011).

Kuk, M., "The Governmental Role in the Making of Chaebol in the Industrial Development of South Korea," *Asian Perspective*, 1988, 12(1): 107–33.

Kumho Asiana Group, Group Overview. Available online: http://www.kumhoasiana.com/kumho_en/SubMain.asp?pgm_id=KUMHO000003 (accessed 15 November 2011).

Kwon, O. Y., *International Business in Korea: The Evolution of the Market in the Globalization Era*, Cheltenham: Edward Elgar, 2008.

—— *The Korean Economy in Transition: An Institutional Perspective*, Cheltenham: Edward Elgar, 2010.

Kwon, S.-H., D.-K. Rhee, and C.-S. Suh, "Globalization Strategies of South Korean Electronics Companies After the 1997 Asian Financial Crisis," *Asia Pacific Business Review*, 2004, 10(3/4): 422–40.

Lansbury, R. D., C.-S. Suh, and S. H. Kwon, *The Global Korean Motor Industry: The Hyundai Motor Company's Global Strategy*, New York: Routledge, 2007.

Lee, B.-H. and S.-J. Cho, "Merger and Reconfiguring of Hyundai-Kia," paper presented at ninth GERPISA International Conference, Paris, 2001. Available online: http://gerpisa. org/rencontre/9.rencontre/S13Lee-Cho.pdf (accessed 2 December 2011).

Lee, E.-S. and S. Kim, "Best Practices and Performance-Based HR System in Korea," *Seoul Journal of Business*, 2006, 12(1): 3–17.

Lee, H., *Economic History of Korea*, 2nd ed., Seoul: Beobmunsa, 1999, 273–89. 이헌창, 한국경제통사, 제2판, 서울: 법문사.

Lee, H.-C., "Transformation of Employment Practices in Korean Businesses," *International Studies of Management and Organization*, 1999, 28 (4): 26–39.

Lee, J. and J. Slater, "Dynamic Capabilities, Entrepreneurial Rent-seeking and the Investment Development Path: The Case of Samsung," *Journal of International Management*, 2007, 13(3): 241–57.

Lee, J. R., *International Marketing*, 5th ed., Seoul: Muyeok Kyongyongsa, 2008. 이장로, 국제마케팅, 제5판, 서울: 무역경영사.

Lee, J. R. and M. Shin, *International Business*, 3rd ed., Seoul: Hongmoonsa, 2008. 이장로, 신만수, 국제경영, 제3판, 서울: 홍문사.

Lee, K. and X. He, "The Capability of the Samsung Group in Project Execution and Vertical Integration: Created in Korea, Replicated in China," *Asian Business and Management*, 2009, 8 (3): 277–99.

Lee, K. and C. H. Lee, "The Miracle to Crisis and the Mirage of the Postcrisis Reform in Korea: Assessment after Ten Years," *Journal of Asian Economics*, 2008, 19(5/6): 425–37.

Lee, K., C. Lim, and W. Song, "Emerging Digital Technology as a Window of Opportunity and Technological Leapfrogging," *International Journal of Technology Management*, 2005, 29(1/2): 40–63.

Lee, K., M. W. Peng, and K. Lee, "From Diversification Premium to Diversification Discount during Institutional Transitions," *Journal of World Business*, 2008, 43(1): 47–65.

Lee, W. and N. S. Lee, "Understanding Samsung's Diversification Strategy: The Case of Samsung Motors Inc," *Long Range Planning*, 2007, 40(4/5): 488–504.

Lee, Y.-I., "South Korean Companies in Transition: an Evolving Strategic Management Style," *Strategic Change*, 2004, 13(1): 29–35.

LG Corporation, About LG: Vision, Management Principles. Available online: http://www.lg.co.kr/about/vision_pop.jsp?num=1 (accessed 17 November 2011). LG 주식회사, LG 소개: 비전, 경영이념.

—— *Passion for Customers, Challenging the Future: 60 Year History of LG*, Seoul: LG Corporation, 2007. 주식회사LG, 고객에대한 열정, 미래를 향한도전, 서울: 주식회사LG.

LG Electronics, About LG: LG's Innovative R&D Efforts Reflect 'Your Dreams'. Available online: http://www.lgcommercial.eu/about-lg (accessed 21 September 2011).

—— Company Overview, 2010 Brochure. Available online: http://www.lg.com/global/ir/company-information/overview.jsp (accessed 13 November 2011).

—— Korea Invest Forum Presentation. Available online: http://www.lg.com/global/ir/reports/other-presentations.jsp (accessed 7 November 2011).

Lotte Group, Business areas. Available online: http://www.lotte.co.kr/english/s2_business/businessarea.html (accessed 15 November 2011).

MacDuffie, J. P. and F. K. Pil, "Changes in Auto Industry Employment Practices: An International Overview" in T. A. Kochan, R. D. Lansbury, and J. P. MacDuffie (eds), *After Lean Production: Evolving Employment Practices in the World Auto Industry*, Ithaca, NY: Cornell University Press, 1997, 9–42.

Mcnamara, D., "The Keishō and the Korean Business Elite," *Journal of Asian Studies*, 1989, 48 (2): 310–23.

Maeil Business, "Putin Personally Congratulates at Opening Ceremony of Hyundai Motor's Factory in Russia," 24 September 2010. 푸틴이 직접축하한 현대차 공장 준공식, 매일경제.

—— "Analyzing Samsung's Five Future Growth Businesses," 12 May 2010. "삼성, 5개 신수종사업 들여다 보니", 매일경제.

Michael Bourne's book *Thoth: Where the Paranormal Meets Mind*. Korean Mythology. Available online: http://www.book-of-thoth.com/thebook/index.php/Korean_mythology#The_Sun_and_the_Moon (accessed 7 November 2011).

Michell, A., *Samsung Electronics and the Struggle for Leadership in the Electronics Industry*, Singapore: Wiley, 2010.

Ministry of Education, Science and Technology, Statistics Service. Available online: http://std.kedi.re.kr/index.jsp (accessed 18 November 2011).

Ministry of Employment and Labor, MOEL Survey Data, Survey on Labor Conditions by Type of Employment. Available online: http://www.moel.go.kr/english/statistics/MOL_Survey_Data.jsp (accessed 18 November 2011).

Moon, I., "Korea's Shipbuilding Industry Sails Ahead," Business Week, 12 May 2006.

Morden, T. and D. Bowles, "Management in South Korea: a Review," *Management Decision*, 1998, 36(5): 316–30.

NCsoft, About Us: History. Available online: http://global.ncsoft.com/global/aboutus/milestone.aspx (accessed 14 November 2011).

—— IR Presentation September 2011. Available online: http://global.ncsoft.com/global/board/downloadlist.aspx?BID=ir_pr (accessed 14 November 2011).

OECD – Organization for Economic Co-operation and Development, *Education at a Glance 2011: OECD Indicators*, Paris: OECD Publishing, 2011.

—— Labour Force Statistics, Summary Tables. Available online: http://stats.oecd.org/ BrandedView.aspx?oecd_bv_id=lfs-data-en&doi=lfs-lfs-data-en (accessed 18 November 2011).

—— *Main Science and Technology Indicators*, Paris: OECD Publishing, 2011.

—— OECD Statistical Extracts: Average Annual Hours Actually Worked per Worker. Available online: http://stats.oecd.org/Index.aspx?DataSetCode=ANHRS (accessed 17 November 2011).

Oh, T. K., "Understanding Managerial Values and Behavior among the Gang of Four: South Korea, Taiwan, Singapore and Hong Kong," *Journal of Management Development*, 1991, 10 (2): 46–56.

Oh, T. K. and E. Kim, "The Impact of Confucianism on East Asian Business Enterprises" in Z. Rhee and E. Chang (eds), *Korean Business and Management: the Reality and the Vision, Elizabeth*, NJ: Hollym, 2002, 207–25.

OICA – International Organization of Motor Vehicle Manufacturers, World Ranking of Manufacturers, Year 2010. Available online: http://oica.net/wp-content/uploads/ranking-2010.pdf (accessed 7 November 2011).

Paik, Y. and Y. S. Park, "The Changing Face of Korean Management of Overseas Affiliates" in C. Rowley and Y. Paik (eds), *The Changing Face of Korean Management*, Oxon: Routledge, 2009, 165–88.

Park, G.-S. and A. E. Kim, "Changes in Attitude toward Work and Workers' Identity in Korea," *Korea Journal*, 2005, 45 (3): 36–57.

Park, W.-S. and G.-C. Yu, "HRM in Korea: Transformation and New Patterns" in Z. Rhee and E. Chang (eds), *Korean Business and Management: the Reality and the Vision*, Elisabeth, NJ: Hollym, 2002, 367–91.

Park, Y., J. Shintaku, J. Tomita, P. Hong, and G. Moon, "Modularity of Flat Panel Display TV and Operation Management Practices: A Case Study of LG Electronics," MMRC Discussion Paper Series No. 248, Tokyo: Manufacturing Management Research Center, 2009.

Peng, H., "The History of SM Entertainment's Growing Empire." Youth Voices. Available online: http://youthvoices.net/discussion/history-sm-entertainments-growing-empire (accessed 14 November 2011).

Plafker, T., *Doing Business in China: How to Profit in the World's Fastest Growing Market*, New York: Warner Business Books, 2007.

POSCO, Posco 3.0 Global Symphony: Posco Sustainability Report 2009. Available online: http://www.posco.co.kr/homepage/docs/kor2/dn/sustain/customer/2009_SR_eng.pdf (accessed 16 November 2011).

Principal Voices round-table, Beijing, May 16, 2005. Available online: http://www. principalvoices.com/beijing.html (accessed 12 November 2011).

Pucik, V. and J.-C. Lim, "Transforming Human Resource Management in a Korean Chaebol: A Case Study of Samsung" in C. Rowley, T.-W. Sohn, and J. Bae (eds), *Managing Korean Business: Organization, Culture, Human Resources and Change*, London: Frank Cass, 2002, 137–60.

Renshaw, J. R., *Korean Women Managers and Corporate Culture: Changing Tradition, Choosing Empowerment, Creating Change*, Oxon: Routledge, 2011.

Roth, K. and A. J. Morrison, "An Empirical Analysis of the Integration-Responsiveness Framework in Global Industries," *Journal of International Business Studies*, 1990, 21(4): 541–64.

Rowley, C. and J. Bae, "Globalization and Transformation of Human Resource Management in South Korea," *International Journal of Human Resource Management*, 2002, 13(3): 522–49.

Rowley, C., J. Bae, and T. W. Sohn, "Introduction: Capabilities to Liabilities in Korean Management" in C. Rowley, T.-W. Sohn, and J. Bae (eds), *Managing Korean Business: Organization, Culture, Human Resources and Change*, London: Frank Cass, 2002, 1–21.

SAJ – The Shipbuilders' Association of Japan, Shipbuilding Statistics, September 2011. Available online: http://www.sajn.or.jp/e/statistics/Shipbuilding_Statistics_Sep2011e. pdf (accessed 7 November 2011).

Samsung Chairman Secretariat Office, *60 Year History of Samsung*, Seoul: Samsung Chairman Secretariat Office, 1998. 삼성회장비서실, 삼성60년사, 서울: 삼성회장비 서실.

Samsung Electronics, *40 Years of Samsung Electronics: the Legacy of Challenge and Creativity*, Suwon: Samsung Electronics Corp., 2010. 삼성전자주식회사: 삼성전자 40년: 도전과창조의 유산, 수원: 삼성전자주식회사.

—— Annual Report 2010. Available online: http://www.samsung.com/us/aboutsamsung/ ir/financialinformation/annualreport/downloads/2010/SECAR2010_Eng_Final.pdf (accessed 7 November 2011).

—— Global R&D Network. Available online: http:/ /www.samsung.com/hk_en/ aboutsamsung/companyprofile/researchanddevelopment/CompanyProfile_Global_RD_ Network.html (accessed 21 September 2011).

—— Samsung Integrity Management. Available online: http://www.samsung.com/sec/ aboutsamsung/Sustainability/integritymanagement.html (accessed 18 November 2011). 삼성전자, Samsung 정도경영.

—— The R&D Workforce & Organization. Available online: http://www.samsung.com/ hk_en/aboutsamsung/companyprofile/researchanddevelopment/CompanyProfile_RD_ WorkforceOrganization.html (accessed 5 September 2011).

Shim, W.-S. and R. M. Steers, "The Entrepreneurial Basis of Korean Enterprise: Past Accomplishments and Future Challenges," *Asia Pacific Business Review*, 2001, 7 (4): 22–43.

Shin, J. S. and S.-W. Jang, *Creating First-Mover Advantages: The Case of Samsung Electronics*, SCAPE Working Paper No. 2005/13, Department of Economics, National University of Singapore, 2005.

SK Corporate Culture Office, *A Journey of Ambition and Intelligence: 50 Years of SK*, Seoul: SK Corporate Culture Office, 2006. SK기업문화실, 패기와 지성의 여정: SK 50년, 서울: SK기업문화실.

Small and Medium Business Administration, Survey Statistics System. Available online: http://stat2.smba.go.kr/dbsearch_re_01.jsp (accessed 7 November 2011). 중소기업청, 조사통계시스템.

SM Entertainment, About Us. Available online: http://www.smtown.com/ir/main.aspx (accessed 14 November 2011).

Song, J.-A, "South Korean Bosses Strive for a Global View," Financial Times, 13 November 2008.

Sorensen, C. W., "Success and Education in Korea," *Comparative Education Review*, 1994, 38 (1): 10–35.

Southerton, D., "Samsung Group Court Ruling Upheld," Korea Legal.org, 31 May 2009. Available online: http://www.koreaexpertwitness.com/blog/uncategorized/120/ (accessed 18 November 2011).

Statistics Agency Korea, *Change of the Korean Economy and Society over 50 Years from a Statistical Viewpoint*, Seoul: Statistics Agency, 1998. 통계로 본 대한민국 50년의 경 제사회상 변화, 서울: 통계청.

Steers, R. M., *Made in Korea: Chung Ju Yung and the Rise of Hyundai*, New York and London: Routledge, 1999.

Steers, R. M., Y. K. Shin, and G. R. Ungson, *The Chaebol: Korea's New Industrial Might*, New York: Ballinger, 1989.

Trim, P. R. J. and Y.-I. Lee, "Insights from Teaching Japanese and Korean Students using Group Work and Case Studies" in D. Saunders and N. Smalley (eds), *The International Gaming and Simulation Research Yearbook*, London: Kogan Page, 2000, 113–24.

Ungson, G. R., R. M. Steers, and S.-H. Park, *Korean Enterprise: The Quest for Globalization*, Boston: Harvard Business School Press, 1997.

Vogel, E., *Japan as Number One: Lessons for America*, Cambridge, MA: Harvard University Press, 1979.

Wang, Y., M. N. Nam, and C.-S. Suh, "Firm Internationalization and Subsidiary Roles: The Case of Hyundai Motor Company," paper presented at the 4th World Congress of Korean Studies, Seoul, 21–24 September 2008.

Whitehall, K., "Samsung Mobile Phones," Author palace. Available online: http://www.authorpalace.com/technology/cell-phones/samsung-mobile-phones.html (accessed 15 September 2011).

Womack, J. P., D. T. Jones, and D. Roos, *The Machine that Changed the World*, Rawson Associates: New York, 1990.

Yang, I., "Jeong Exchange and Collective Leadership in Korean Organizations," *Asia Pacific Journal of Management*, 2006, 23(3): 283–98.

Yee, J., "The Social Networks of Koreans," *Korea Journal*, 2000, 40(1): 325–52.

YTN News, "Job Generation through Co-prosperity is Social Policy, says President Lee Myung-bak," 14 September 2010. 이명박 대통령 "동반성장 통한 일자리 창출이 서민 정책", YTN 뉴스.

Yu, G.-C. and C. Rowley, "The Changing Face of Korean Human Resource Management" in C. Rowley and Y. Paik (eds), *The Changing Face of Korean Management*, Oxon: Routledge, 2009, 29–51.

Index